WITHDRAWAL

NEW AMERICAN SCHOOLS' CONCEPT OF BREAK THE MOLD DESIGNS

How Designs Evolved and Why

Susan Bodilly

RAND
EDUCATION

Supported by
New American Schools

The research described in this report was supported by New American Schools.

Library of Congress Cataloging-in-Publication Data

Bodilly, Susan J.
 New American Schools' concept of break-the-mold designs : how designs
evolved and why / Susan Bodilly.
  p. cm.
  "MR-1288-NAS."
  Includes bibliographical references.
  ISBN 0-8330-2932-0
  1. New American Schools (Organization) 2. School improvement programs—
United States—Evaluation. 3. Educational change—United States. I. Title.

LB2822.82 .B638 2001
379.1'5—dc21

                                                              00-068399

RAND is a nonprofit institution that helps improve policy and decisionmaking through research and analysis. RAND® is a registered trademark. RAND's publications do not necessarily reflect the opinions or policies of its research sponsors.

Published 2001 by RAND
1700 Main Street, P.O. Box 2138, Santa Monica, CA 90407-2138
1200 South Hayes Street, Arlington, VA 22202-5050
RAND URL: http://www.rand.org/
To order RAND documents or to obtain additional information,
contact Distribution Services: Telephone: (310) 451-7002;
Fax: (310) 451-6915; Internet: order@rand.org

New American Schools (NAS), also known as New American Schools Development Corporation (NASDC) from 1991 to 1995, is a private nonprofit corporation created in conjunction with President Bush's America 2000 initiative. Its purpose is to fund design teams to develop and disseminate whole-school designs for elementary and secondary schools. NAS's goal is to ensure that these designs, presumably offering more effective educational programs than in typical schools, are adopted in schools across the country so as to significantly improve student performance. Since its inception NAS has completed a development phase, a demonstration phase, and a scale-up phase.

During these phases (1992–2000) RAND provided analytic support to NAS that resulted in the RAND publications cited below. This report documents an analysis of the changes made by 1998 to the original 1992 designs and design teams. The report is targeted toward educational policymakers interested in comprehensive school reform and others interested in improving the likelihood of implementation of reform efforts in local governmental bureaucracies. The research was supported by NAS with funding from the Ford Foundation and an anonymous donor. The study was completed under the auspices of RAND Education. The RAND reports include:

Designing New American Schools: Baseline Observations on Nine Design Teams, Susan J. Bodilly, Susanna Purnell, Kimberly Ramsey, and Christina Smith, MR-598-NASDC, 1995.

Lessons from New American Schools Development Corporation's Demonstration Phase, Susan Bodilly, MR-729-NASDC, 1996.

Reforming and Conforming: NASDC Principals Discuss School Accountability Systems, Karen J. Mitchell, MR-716-NASDC, 1996.

New American Schools After Six Years, Thomas K. Glennan, Jr., MR-945-NAS, 1998.

Lessons from New American Schools' Scale-Up Phase: Prospects for Bringing Designs to Multiple Schools, Susan J. Bodilly, MR-942-NAS, 1998.

"Funding Comprehensive School Reform," Brent Keltner, IP-175, 1998.

Assessing the Progress of New American Schools: A Status Report, Mark Berends, MR-1085-EDU, 1999.

Implementation and Performance in New American Schools: Three Years into Scale-Up, Mark Berends, Sheila Kirby, Scott Naftel, and Christopher McKelvey, MR-1145-EDU, 2001.

CONTENTS

FIGURES

TABLES

Business leaders created New American Schools, a private nonprofit corporation, in 1991 to develop "break-the-mold" designs for schools serving grades K–12. The notion of a design was meant to convey a *coherent* and *comprehensive* set of school-level practices that unified a school behind a goal of high performance by all students. These practices would cover all grades, all students in the school, and all important functional areas of the school.

The founders of NAS sought both to support the development of designs by design teams and to ensure the designs were adopted or adapted throughout the country by schools seeking to transform themselves. Adoption would be supported by assistance provided by the design teams associated with each design. Since this beginning, NAS as an organization has changed significantly (Glennan, 1998). In addition, the designs developed by NAS and the teams have changed significantly as they have tried to implement their designs in hundreds of schools in ten districts that partnered with NAS for this purpose. These changes to designs are the subject of this report.

PURPOSE AND METHODS

The literature on educational reform indicates that changes to interventions such as designs will occur for multiple reasons, most especially because educational reforms are embedded in complex political systems of actors with limited capacity and will to change. Interactions between these actors as they seek to implement the design will cause the intervention to be reshaped or adapted to fit this environment. Sometimes changes to the intervention are beneficial; they result in stronger implementation and stronger effects. Often they are not; adaptations can result in weak implementation of original concepts and weak effects.

So far, evaluations of the NAS designs show only modest implementation of the NAS designs in scale-up districts chosen by NAS and only modest improvements in student performance in these districts (Bodilly, 1998; Berends et al., 2001). These results have several possible explanations: (1) the designs when implemented do not have the strong effects desired; (2) the designs were weakly implemented so as to have only modest effects; (3) the design concept itself changed, not necessarily for the better, during the demonstration and scale-up phases.

The purpose of this report is to document changes to the designs over their short life span and reasons for those changes to better understand the likely contribution of this reform to student improvements. We used historical analysis of the design documents, interviews with design teams, and notes from site visits to establish the changes that have taken place in designs over the period 1992 to 1998. We used the original proposals submitted in response to NAS's Request for Proposals as the baseline for making comparisons. This might overestimate the changes made because proposals often overpromise the interventions to be developed in order to gain favor in a competitive environment.

FINDINGS

We found significant changes over time in the designs and in the concept of what a design included. NAS drove some of these changes in its decisions to fund or not to fund specific designs. The designs themselves have changed in terms of their educational components and theories. Finally, the design teams have developed implementation strategies and assistance packages over time that have resulted in the expansion of the design concept to the concept of "design-based assistance." The following sections summarize the major changes.

NAS Portfolio and Strategy Changes

Funding concerns drove the reduction in number of design teams and designs. These changes can bee seen as unplanned and necessitated by unpredictable events that overtook the funder and, therefore, the teams. Two teams were led by districts dedicated to local efforts at reform; they suffered from unplanned, slow design development connected to political problems due to the teams' base in local governance. Four teams, including these two district-led teams, did not demonstrate the ability or interest to move outside their local areas in the scale-up phase. NAS chose to eliminate three of these design teams and designs as unsuitable for scale-up and did not promote the fourth in NAS districts. The lesson NAS learned is that design teams could not be embedded in local government or they would be embroiled in local politics to the exclusion of development of the design.

Decisions leading to the scale-up phase indicated a growing understanding by NAS of the difficulties of school reform and how the school-based design concept had to be embedded in larger systemic reforms. NAS pushed the design teams to expand in ten jurisdictions that NAS chose, based on the jurisdictions' claims about their ability to support designs. With this strategy the success of the teams and their designs were then dependent on the joint action of themselves, NAS, and the multiple players in the partner jurisdictions. These jurisdictions were mostly large urban districts with significant populations of students from families living in poverty.

Changes to Designs

The analysis found that most design teams changed individual elements or components of their designs gradually over time. We categorized the changes as: planned development; response to the needs of students and teachers in the schools served; adaptation to conflicting policies, rules, and regulation in the jurisdictions; and complete reconceptualization of the design or specific elements. In general we found that all designs had experienced some planned development, but they also experienced unforeseen adaptations.

The experiences of going to scale in large, urban districts with high percentages of low-income families led to significant changes within the designs as they adapted to the needs of students and teachers in these schools. In particular, the adoption or development of basic literacy and numeracy programs and the development of processes to train teachers to develop rubrics for assessing student work against state or district standards became necessary. Lack of teacher time, motivation, or capacity led to significant changes in designs. Teams responded to this lack by further developing their assistance packages, reducing the need for teacher-developed materials and curriculum, and reducing the need for teacher-led activities.

Teams gradually adapted the designs significantly in response to the pressures posed by states, districts, schools, and unions to meet the existing regulatory environment. The accommodating stance taken by most design teams in newer versions of their design documents allows significant variation in sites associated with a single team. Some design documents now indicate that schools are considered to be implementing the design when they combine state standards (with state tests that are not aligned to the other design elements) and use an ad hoc mix of design and district curriculum and instruction. This lack of a strong stance on the core functions of the school can allow significant fragmentation, rather than cohesion, in the design-based schools. The major exception to the gradual adaptation seen is the National Alliance for Restructuring Education (NARE) design, which did not gradually adapt to districts' demands but in 1999 was entirely reconceptualized to better meet the needs of teachers in schools. The Roots and Wings (RW) team made fewer changes than most teams to its design.

Development of Implementation Strategies

Over several years implementation assistance has grown considerably to include a selection process, specified committee structures, task forces, and learning groups within schools, as well as formal assistance packages including training programs, and the beginnings of a quality control system. The manner of growth has been influenced by both the needs of teachers and the policy stances of districts.

Design teams have focused on these teacher needs and have attempted to develop assistance packages to support school staff. District demands for immediate results, while failing to provide resources dedicated to professional development, incentives for teacher sharing, and policies to discourage rapid turnover of teachers in schools, have undermined the design teams' assistance strategies to provide time to teachers for reform. The implication is that design-based assistance works only if schools have slack resources for reform, which often depends on district policy and was missing in several districts in the scale-up phase.

The teams have made strides in quality assurance through the significant development of benchmarks, which came about at least in part as an adaptation to the demands by districts and teachers. But districts have also limited the furtherance of the quality assurance function because of their strong stance on mandated tests as the sole indicator upon which teams will be judged. These tests might not align well with the performance standards, curriculum, or instruction proposed by teams.

POLICY IMPLICATIONS

NAS began with a working hypothesis that comprehensive designs would bring unity and cohesion to schools, which would in turn improve student outcomes. This cohesion was in part predicated upon the notion that designs themselves would provide a package of well thought out and aligned standards, assessments, curriculum, instructional strategies, and professional development plans. Some of the changes made to designs were beneficial in promoting the concept of a design-based school, especially the development of stronger curriculum packages, the development of clear descriptions of the designs, and significant work toward assistance for schools to adopt designs. However, concessions to district and state policies led design teams to redefine some design elements, allowing significant local variation and possible incoherence and fragmentation within schools using designs.

The federal government recently has embraced the notion of comprehensive school reform through changes in its Title I regulations and by providing funds for schools adopting designs such as those supported by NAS through the Comprehensive School

Reform Demonstration program (CSRD). Significant numbers of schools throughout the country are now adopting designs under CSRD. Some are NAS sponsored; many are not. The assumption behind this legislation is the same as that behind NAS: coherent designs combined with external assistance providers will enable schools to significantly improve their students' performance. This further assumes some notion of coherence of designs, strong implementation support and reasoned implementation strategies, and resulting performance when federal financial assistance is provided.

This report indicates these are not reasonable expectations, for NAS designs or for others that will adapt to the same types of environments. If this reform is to succeed, then policymakers must revitalize it by taking this current environment into account and helping to make the environment more supportive. Clearly, NAS, a small business-oriented organization, cannot do this by itself; the revitalization requires substantial effort by the public bodies that govern schools. The federal government and others such as NAS should consider ways in which to rejuvenate the design concept so as to really promote comprehensive reforms. They must find ways to protect designs from further retreating from important education principles; help designs develop implementation strategies to support teachers; and help districts and states adopt policies that support designs.

ACKNOWLEDGMENTS

The author wishes to acknowledge the many people who have made this research possible. New American Schools requested and supported the research. Two foundations provided funding and encouragement for the work: the Ford Foundation and an anonymous donor. Design teams provided documents, their time, and expertise. District representatives and school-level administrators and staff also provided their time in the course of this study. I thank all of the above for their help in this work.

Within RAND several colleagues were essential to completion of the study: Tom Glennan, Kimberly Gavin, and Mark Berends. The reviewers, Carol Weiss of Harvard University and Tora Bikson of RAND, provided constructive criticism and suggestions that greatly improved the document.

AC	Audrey Cohen College of Education, now Purpose Centered Education: The Audrey Cohen College System of Education
ATLAS	Authentic Teaching, Learning and Assessment for All Students
CLC	Community Learning Centers
CON	CoNect
CSRD	Comprehensive School Reform Demonstration
ELOB	Expeditionary Learning/Outward Bound
IEC/IEP	Individual Education Compact/Individual Education Plan
LAEP	Los Angeles Educational Partnership
LALC	Los Angeles Learning Centers
LRDC	Learning Research and Development Center
MRSH	Modern Red Schoolhouse
MSPAP	Maryland School Performance Assessment Program
NARE	National Alliance for Restructuring Education
NAS	New American Schools

NASDC	New American Schools Development Corporation
RFP	Request for Proposals
RW	Roots and Wings
TAAS	Texas Assessment of Academic Skills
TQM	Total Quality Management
ULC	Urban Learning Centers (formerly Los Angeles Learning Centers)

Chapter One

INTRODUCTION

This introductory chapter provides the motivation for this study, discussing our purposes and research questions and providing background on New American Schools important for understanding the report. The literature on implementation and its implications is reviewed. Then the chapter describes the methods used and lays out the organization of the remainder of the report.

NEW AMERICAN SCHOOLS' PURPOSES AND POLICY IMPORTANCE

New American Schools (NAS, also known as New American Schools Development Corporation [NASDC]) represents a response to the call for more "systemic reform" and more "standards-based reform." That call was firmly pronounced at the National Governors' Summit on Education in 1988, reiterated in 1991 by President Bush in his America 2000 initiative, and again by President Clinton in his Education 2000 initiative. All three called for the transformation or reinvention of American schools to meet the needs of children in the 21st century.

At the urging of President Bush, business leaders created NAS, a private nonprofit corporation, in 1991 to fund design teams to develop "break-the-mold" designs for schools in grades K–12. NAS's ultimate purpose is to improve student performance throughout the United States by developing effective designs and helping schools to adopt those designs. It sent out a broad Request for Proposals (RFP) for design teams to submit designs for break-the-mold schools. These design teams were groups of interested parties from universities, school districts, public sector agencies, nonprofit consulting firms, and the private sector. Some existed before the NAS effort; others sprang up in response to it. The design teams chosen from the competitive process were to each: (1) develop a comprehensive design for schools; (2) test the design's effectiveness in demonstration sites; and (3) ensure the designs were adopted by schools throughout the country by the provision of "design assistance" services during a scale-up phase.

The NAS notion of a school design was a coherent set of school-level practices that unified a school behind a goal of high student performance by all students. These practices would cover all grades and all students in the school. In addition, they would cover important functional areas of the school: standards, assessment, curriculum, instruction, professional development, student assignment, governance, etc. As indicated in the original RFP calling for school designers to apply, "This is an effort to integrate all elements of a school's life" (NASDC, 1991, p. 20). Because of this global coverage, the designs were referred to as comprehensive or whole-school to distinguish them from other reform ideas that were targeted at only one or two functional areas or selected groups of students.

The NAS initiative took hold and has continued for almost a decade with teams developing, testing, marketing, and providing assistance for adopting their designs. These teams spread their designs throughout the country to approximately 1,500 schools by 1999. This number includes all schools that have ever joined in partnership with an NAS design without regard to actual levels of implementation of the design or current status. As developed, the notion of design and design team goes hand in hand. Each design team has acted as developer, tester, marketer, and assistance provider for its unique design. When NAS and others talk about this initiative they often use the terms *designs* and *design teams* interchangeably—the two have become largely inseparable in people's minds.

The NAS initiative has influenced federal policy, and federal policy has influenced its growth. Federal Title I legislation opened up a potential market for designs: Title I funds are allocated to schools serving high proportions of at-risk students, usually defined as students receiving free or reduced-price lunches. Past legislation had dictated that these students be served separately from non-at-risk students, resulting in "pull-out" programs in schools. However, since 1994 a series of changes in federal regulations has enabled some Title I schools to no longer separate students but to use the federal funds across the entire school population. These approaches are known as Title I school-wide programs. Now any school with more than 50 percent at-risk students can use its Title I funds for school-wide programs. Comprehensive school designs are an acceptable use of the funds, and so some schools have used Title I school-wide funds to pay for design teams and their services.

In 1997, the U.S. Congress passed appropriation language that provided for funding to schools attempting to undertake comprehensive or whole-school designs. The Obey-Porter legislation, known as the Comprehensive School Reform Demonstration Program (CSRD), offers schools a minimum of $50,000 per year for three years to adopt designs.[1] Eight NAS designs along with about ten others are prominently featured in the conference report. The first awards were made in the 1998–1999 school year. Enough funding was provided to allow for approximately 2,500 schools to adopt designs over a three-year period. Thus, a potential new market opened up for the design teams.

This environment has promoted expansion of designs and design-based assistance in schools throughout the country using federal funding. District- and state-level funds have also been used to pay for the design teams' work in schools. The public nature of the funds and the designs' application to public schools underscores the need to understand the nature and effectiveness of designs in promoting improved student achievement.

RAND has promoted this understanding by analyzing both the level of implementation evident in the different phases of NAS and the effects of adoption on student performance (Bodilly, 1998; Keltner, 1998; Berends, 1999; Berends et al., 2001). RAND has found that implementation has lagged behind the expectations set by NAS, with

_____

[1]http://www.ed.gov/offices/OESE/compreform.

approximately half the schools studied showing strong implementation and others lagging behind (Bodily, 1998).

RAND has also shown that in schools associated with NAS's scale-up strategy test score results have not shown, on average, dramatic increases in performance (Berends et al., 2000). This is not surprising given the level of implementation observed in many schools. Analysis by American Institutes for Research (AIR, 1999) of all the research on effects of designs shows few designs can claim strong student effects. Of the 24 designs included in its report, including all the NAS designs, only a handful of designs had ever had rigorous evaluations of their activities, and those with rigorous evaluations often showed ambiguous student outcomes. A recent series of articles in *Education Researcher* and *Phi Delta Kappan* presents results specific to Success for All (the reading component of a NAS design) and follows a debate between Robert Slavin and Stanley Pogrow as to the meaning of the results (Slavin, 1997a, 1997b, 1999, 2000; Pogrow, 1998, 2000). This debate indicates some of the reasons why results are so inconclusive.

RAND has written several volumes on the reasons behind these types of findings concerning NAS designs. Omitted from those volumes is a clear discussion of how the designs and teams have changed over time in ways that might have contributed to these results or have actually improved the results from what they might otherwise have been.

PURPOSE OF THE STUDY

As part of its assessment of NAS, RAND has tracked the changes made in design teams and in designs, attempting to understand the changing nature of the intervention being developed. Changes in the designs and teams were expected for several reasons, not least of which was that the effort as a whole was *planned* to be developmental with different stages of *planned* development for the designs. In addition, a long history of implementation of education reform in this country points to the probability that the designs would adapt in *unplanned* ways in response to demonstration and implementation experiences.

Our observation from assessing the NAS initiative over a nine-year period is that indeed the designs and teams have changed in important substantive ways, both planned and unplanned. We think the processes of change and reasons for these changes are important for education policymakers to understand. The history of the transformation of the designs from simple ideas on paper to highly developed products provides insight into the manner in which the educational policy environment often transmutes reforms in strange ways—sometimes into stronger ideas, sometimes into weak substitutes, and sometimes into a mist of confusion or drift.

This report, historical in nature, addresses three issues, each focused on the evolution of the concept of a design and the provision of design-based assistance services by design teams:

- How have the designs changed since their conception? We wish to chronicle the various types of changes that have occurred in designs since the original proposals, thus enabling a more concrete understanding of the solidity and permanency of the concept of a "comprehensive, whole-school design."

- What has caused changes to the designs? We wish to identify reasons for those changes to increase our understanding of how designs interacted within the system in which they worked.

- What lessons can be learned from NAS design team experiences that can help other teams or the federal effort to promote effective comprehensive school reform? We wish to draw policy implications from the process of change that NAS and its designs have undergone.

We have chosen the concept of a design as the unit of analysis. NAS itself could be considered the intervention of interest and deserves a similar type of analysis. In addition, design teams could be considered the intervention, though teams and design often cannot be separated easily for distinct analysis. But the purpose of this report is to focus on the NAS concept of design as embedded in its teams' designs and how that concept has changed over time.

NAS BACKGROUND

The founders of NAS sought to both develop designs and see them adopted or adapted throughout the country by schools seeking to transform or reinvent themselves. NAS held a competition through an RFP and received more than 600 proposals from existing teams in universities, districts attempting reforms, and newly formed teams from private nonprofit and for-profit groups. NAS imposed several conditions on the designs and their associated teams:

- In creating designs, teams should not be limited by the constraints facing "real" schools in real districts, but rather let their imaginations develop truly innovative and provocative ideas.

- Designs had to enable all students to meet high standards. Designs geared toward a particular subgroup were not acceptable.

- The design should be adaptable to local circumstances. As stated in the proposal, "This is not a request to establish 'model' schools. The designs must be adaptable so that they can be used by many communities to create their own new schools" (NASDC, 1991, p. 21).

- While it was accepted that the designs would require funds to implement in a real school, the long-term costs of operating a design-based school should not be greater than that for operating an average school.

- Teams had to commit to a scale-up phase starting in 1995 during which they would promote their design in schools across the country. A specific criterion for judging designs was "potential for widespread application and the quality of plans for fostering such application" (NASDC, 1991, p. 35).

NAS DESIGN TEAMS

NAS selected these 11 proposals for funding:

Authentic Teaching, Learning, and Assessment for All Students— ATLAS was proposed by a team headed jointly by Ted Sizer, Howard

Gardner, James Comer, and Janet Whitla. The design assumed that high-performing schools were not possible in the current bureaucratic structure. The design aimed to change the culture of the school to promote high institutional and individual performance through (1) helping students acquire valuable habits of heart, mind, and work; (2) helping students develop deep understanding; (3) using only activities that are developmentally appropriate; and (4) creating a community of learners. The design required the establishment of a semi-autonomous feeder pattern of high school, middle school, and elementary schools and significant development of a committee structure within schools and across schools. It did not prescribe standards or curriculum.

Audrey Cohen College—AC (now called Purpose Centered Education: The Audrey Cohen College System of Education) was proposed by the College for Human Services in New York City. It emphasized adoption of a developmentally appropriate, transdisciplinary curriculum based on semester-long units focused on particular purposes for learning—not subject area. For example, kindergarten was dedicated to "We build a family and school partnership" and "We care for living things." Embedded in each purpose were content areas and essential skills. Semester-long purposes were to be generated by the design team along with significant guidance for curriculum development, but teachers developed their own curriculum. Each purpose culminated in a constructive action taken by the class to serve the community. These purposes and actions become the guiding principles for the organization of the school.

Bensenville New American Schools Project—The Bensenville project was proposed by the Bensenville School district in Illinois by a team that included union members, government leaders, business owners, parents, and others. It called for a complete rethinking of the classroom so that the entire community would serve as a campus. The instruction would be hands-on and project-based, taking place at sites throughout the community. A Lifelong Learning Center would provide assessments of all community members' health and learning needs.

CoNect—CON was proposed by the private for-profit firm of Bolt, Beranek, and Newman with support from other partners such as

Boston College. It focused on creating a school environment through the ubiquitous use of technology that would motivate children through interdisciplinary projects that extended outside the classroom walls. The design called for autonomy of the school and for planning and budgeting by houses or grade levels within the school.

Community Learning Centers—CLC was proposed by a coalition of education groups led by Public Schools Incentives, a private nonprofit educational group. This design covered children from birth to 21. Based on full school autonomy similar to that provided to charter schools using a contractual vehicle to maintain autonomy and accountability, CLC emphasized project-based learning, authentic assessments, and a student-led curriculum. It called for school-level provision of health and social services in community learning centers.

Expeditionary Learning/Outward Bound—ELOB was proposed by Outward Bound, a private nonprofit organization. It wanted to take the ideas espoused by Outward Bound and apply them to schools, including interdisciplinary field-based curriculum, personalized instruction, and more authentic assessments. Children would be in groups of no more than 25 students per teacher with the same teacher for three years. Schools would have no more than 350 students; teachers would develop their own curriculum.

Los Angeles Learning Centers (LALC), now **Urban Learning Centers**—ULC was proposed by a coalition of the Los Angeles Unified School district, the Los Angeles Educational Partnership (LAEP), UCLA, USC, and others, and it was to be led by LAEP. The design called for the creation of pre-K–12 schools that provided for student educational, health, and social service needs. Each child would have mentors—from the community, other school children, and teachers. Teaching would be thematic and project-based with teachers developing curriculum. The design would develop and use its own standards. Students would be in small groups.

Modern Red Schoolhouse—MRSH was proposed by the Hudson Institute, a private nonprofit organization. The design called for the design team to create new standards, and schools were to adopt Core Knowledge curriculum and use interdisciplinary units developed by teachers. Students would be in multi-age, multi-year groups and have Individual Education Compacts that articulated a personalized education program for each student. Student records would be managed by a school-wide computer system, and teachers would use this to help manage personalized instruction. The school would require complete autonomy from district control and parental choice of school.

National Alliance for Restructuring Education—NARE (now America's Choice) was proposed by the National Center for Education and the Economy in Rochester, New York. The design team of 36 members promised to create new standards for schools that included important workplace skills and were matched to a set of assessments against which student progress toward standards could be measured. The schools would have increased autonomy under districts and states that fundamentally restructured their education provisions, along lines proposed in the Total Quality Management literature. Teachers would develop curriculum and instructional packages after being exposed to best practices. Health and social service resources would be provided at each campus.

Odyssey Project—The design was proposed by the school district of Gaston County in North Carolina. The design team leader was the head of research and development for the district and all team members were employed by the school system with one exception. The design addressed needs of children ages 3–18 with extensive interventions in early years. It proposed year-round schooling, use of specific instructional strategies, a high-technology environment, multi-grade grouping, school-level provision of social services and health care, and required community service. Curriculum and instruction would be "outcomes based" and geared toward developing the multiple intelligences of all students.

Roots and Wings—RW was proposed by the Johns Hopkins Center for Research on Effective Schooling for Disadvantaged Students, St. Mary's Public Schools, and the Department of Education for the State of Maryland. It covered only elementary grades. The roots part of the design would ensure that all children received coordinated, relentless attention to the five core subject areas from birth on. It included the existing Success for All reading program and two new components: one for math and the other for social studies and science. All curricula would be developed by the design team with teachers trained in its use. Schools would provide extended day care, health and family services, tutoring, site-based management, and parental choice.

NAS PHASES AND APPROACH

NAS, with some understanding of the ambitiousness of its goals, used a phased approach to develop the designs from 50-page proposals to functioning designs in multiple schools, as shown in Figure 1.1. These phases include: (1) a one-year development and specification phase; (2) a two-year demonstration where the team had to show that the design could be implemented in at least two real schools; and (3) a scale-up phase where NAS would attempt to move the designs into schools across the country. Over the course of these phases NAS reduced the number of teams to seven actively working in selected jurisdictions with schools to help them adopt the designs from 1995 to 1998.

In 1995, after the completion of the two-year demonstration phase NAS reorganized its activities in support of its mission in several important ways that together became known as the Phase 3 scale-up strategy. Three major themes drove the scale-up phase.

First, in the past NAS had provided funding to the teams to develop the designs and implement them in schools. In total the NAS effort allocated about $120 million in funds up to 1998. Starting with the scale-up phase in Summer 1995, NAS urged the design teams to adopt a "fee-for-service" approach, charging schools and districts for their services. NAS stated it would move away from funding design teams, although it created an entrepreneurial fund to make loans to teams for working capital or investments in product improvements. This notion of fee for service was in keeping with the strong business base and philosophy of NAS.

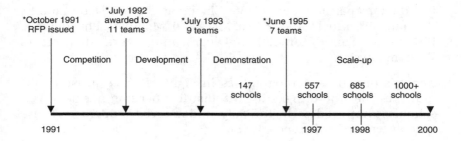

Figure 1.1—NAS Phases

Second, the demonstration phase experience pointed to the importance of the design to schools, but also to the need of schools for ongoing assistance in adopting the designs. Most schools using the design by itself could not transform. Thus, the teams and NAS began to emphasize the designs joined with an implementation assistance package. This product came to be known as "design-based assistance" (Bodilly et al., 1996). The design teams evolved from being "thinkers of break-the-mold concepts" to service providers or assistance organizations. Consonant with the first point, teams began to charge fees for the services and materials they provided such as training of teachers and staff, curriculum units, and conferences.

Third, NAS came to believe, whether through persuasive arguments from systemic reformers or from evidence of the barriers to implementation of designs, that district policies and procedures posed hazards to implementing design-based assistance in schools. Schools could not transform unless supported by districts. Thus, NAS chose a scale-up strategy with two parts: (1) design teams were free to opportunistically pursue contacts and bring schools into their fold; (2) at the same time, NAS itself would begin to work with a limited number of districts to develop "markets" for the designs. These markets would be in jurisdictions supportive of the effort. In particular, NAS sought jurisdictions that would commit to a five-year partnership with NAS and its associated teams to create a supportive environment for whole-school changes. The partnering jurisdictions would also commit to transforming 30 percent of their schools using design-based assistance within a five-year period. The following jurisdictions partnered with NAS: Cincinnati, Miami-Dade County, the state of Kentucky, the state of Maryland, Memphis, Philadelphia, Pittsburgh, San Antonio, San Diego, and several districts in Washington state.

Analysis of school demographics in eight of these jurisdictions indicates that the designs in NAS districts became partners with schools composed of historically underserved students. These schools tend to be (Berends, 1999):

- High-poverty schools—on average 54 percent of students were on free or reduced-lunch compared to 40 percent nationally.

- Largely minority schools—on average about 60 percent of the students were minority compared to 35 percent nationally.

- Low-performing schools—on average schools scored at or below the district average on state tests and the districts were some of the lowest performing districts in their respective states.

In earlier phases NAS did not push designs to increase the numbers of schools they served. Rather it focused its attention on ensuring the designs could be demonstrated in at least a few schools. However, with the move to the scale-up strategy, NAS's emphasis changed to increasing the number of schools that adopted designs. NAS began to push the partner districts to increase the number of schools implementing designs and pushed the designs to increase the number of their schools in these districts.

In October 1998 a new board of directors and new chief executive officer of the board were seated at NAS. The old NAS, whose purpose was to develop designs, is now gone and a new NAS exists to promote design-based assistance and whole-school reform nationwide.

Again NAS is looking to increase the numbers of schools using its designs. It hopes to use Comprehensive School Reform Demonstration (CSRD) funding and the school-wide provisions of Title I to support some of that growth. Meanwhile schools are looking at NAS and other designs trying to understand what this notion called comprehensive school reform can contribute to their improvement and what design-based assistance means.

IMPLICATIONS OF THE LITERATURE

This report will show that the designs have changed significantly over time and that it was reasonable to expect changes. What could not be predicted were the specific changes. To understand this we turn to a brief review of the literature on implementation of educational reforms.

The public sector attempts to improve organizational performance in four different ways: (1) by adding new tasks to the repertoire of an existing organization; (2) by creating a new organization to perform tasks that other existing organizations already do; (3) by creating a new organization to perform new tasks; and (4) by asking an existing organization to significantly alter existing tasks to improve performance (Wilson, 1989).

The fourth case is known as a reform effort—literally to re-form the behaviors and tasks of the existing organization. A reform effort is considered the most difficult type of improvement to accomplish, especially when: (1) multiple levels of government are involved, (2) significantly different behaviors are called for, (3) the tasks and behaviors are those of a large and diverse group, and (4) the participants have varying incentives to change (Mazmanian and Sabatier, 1989).

These conditions apply in the case of comprehensive school reforms. Implementation of a design in a school involves federal, state, and local government, the design team, and multiple other actors. It requires significantly different sets of behaviors for students, teachers, principals, and administrators, and those groups respond to and are driven by many varying incentives other than those offered by a design team (Gitlin and Margonis, 1995; Cuban, 1984 Huberman and Miles, 1984).

A long line of implementation studies directed at school reform indicates that the difficulties arise because:

> Policy makers can't mandate what matters most: local capacity and will. . . . Environmental stability, competing centers of authority, contending priorities or pressures and other aspects of the social-political milieu can influence implementor willingness

profoundly. . . . Change is ultimately a problem of the smallest unit (McLaughlin, 1987, pp. 172–173).

The end result of an implementation stage focused on schools and teacher behaviors is often "mutual adaptation" with local educational agencies, school staff, and intermediaries changing behaviors in unexpected ways (Berman and McLaughlin, 1975). As McLaughlin put it, "Local variability is the rule; uniformity is the exception" (1990, p. 13). The use of the term *mutual adaptation* often invokes a benign process of movement toward mutually agreed to goals with the intervention changing for the better in some sense so as to support those goals.

Others have found that adaptation does not always lead to enhancement of the original policy or necessarily promote the desired performance outcomes. These less benign effects have been categorized in different ways as unanticipated consequence, policy disappearance, policy erosion, policy dilution, policy drift, or simply poor or slowed implementation (Cuban, 1984; Pressman and Wildavsky, 1973; Daft, 1982; Mazmanian and Sabatier, 1989; Weatherley and Lipsky, 1977; Yin, 1979).

These less desirable outcomes often occur because policymakers did not put in place needed support mechanisms. McDonnell and Grubb (1991) make clear that successful implementation of any educational mandate requires support of the implementers, capacity on their part to follow the mandate, and some enforcement or incentives to support compliance. The building of capacity requires the infusion of resources in terms of time, funding, and information—either social or intellectual. These resources are often referred to as "slack" or "slack resources," without which reform cannot be successfully undertaken. Capacity cannot be mandated.

The education literature does point to important supports that, if provided, often lead to implementation closer to that expected by policymakers (fidelity). These conditions include (McLaughlin, 1990):

- Active participation and support of district leadership, including the removal of conflicting priorities and initiatives

- Funding to get the initiative under way and indicate its importance

- Understanding by stakeholders/implementers of the intervention and its intended effects gained through clear communication

- Specific attention to implementation—that is, curricular or instructional programs require substantial effort at getting school-level staff to understand them, adopt them, and use them consistently and effectively.   Some of these supportive implementation strategies might include:

  — Concrete and specific teacher training including classroom assistance by local staff

  — Teacher observations of similar projects in like settings

  — Stakeholder acceptance of the initiative and participation in project decisions and regular project meetings focused on practical issues

  — Local development of project material.

Finally, the literature points to the phenomenon of implementation progression, with full implementation sometimes only evident after several stages of activity (Mazmanian and Sabatier, 1989; Yin, 1979). This phenomenon occurs in part because of the developmental nature of some interventions, but it can also be due to the cycles of political support and interest that come and go depending on the values of leaders in office, competing policy issues, and the funding picture.

These lessons provide insight into what expectations were reasonable for NAS as it proceeded; however, NAS was not necessarily aware of these. Starting in 1991 with the creation of design proposals the following might reasonably be expected:

- The number and emphasis of the teams could be expected to change given their dependence on NAS. As with other efforts of this kind, the livelihood and political fortunes of the parent organization or major funding source would affect the practices of the funding recipients. The development and funding picture of NAS would have an effect on the teams themselves and their ability to meet their vision.

- The designs and their theories of education including their notions of standards, assessment, curriculum, and instruction (Fullan, 1999) could be expected to have significant further planned development over time. NAS chose a developmental approach and expected teams to carefully plan further development needs, such as more fully articulated curriculum packages aligned to more fully developed standards.

- Significant changes to designs and design teams could be expected due to unplanned mutual adaptation during the demonstration and scale-up phases as teams interacted with local districts and schools. Language in the RFP implied that NAS expected the design teams to learn from their experiences in real schools during the first several years and further improve their designs to ensure the final outcomes desired—significant student performance increases. This benign view of mutual adaptation emphasizes that the end product of change would still result in comprehensive and coherent designs leading to improved performance, but that the implementing site's fidelity to the specifics of the design would vary from locale to locale.

- Adaptation to local district politics and prerogatives, poor communication by design teams about their designs, shifts in funding, leadership turnover, and competing priorities could all be expected to lead to design incoherence and fragmentation as teams and schools struggled to make progress. Alternatively, schools might lack the capacity to undertake design-based reforms. School staff might not have the time or capability to comply with the design requirements and without further support might fail in their implementation. This equally plausible scenario was not recognized in the RFP.[2]

---

[2]In a previous report, RAND noted the possibility of these less desirable outcomes (Bodilly, 1998, p. 18):

> . . . Embedded in the NAS approach is a possible conflict. On the one hand, in the RFP, NAS called for "break-the-mold" designs that ignored existing rules, regulations, and traditions governing schools. On the other hand, in demonstration and scale-up, NAS asked for rapid matching and implementation in existing schools that face very real rules, regulations and

- While the RFP asked for implementation strategies, few teams focused on these in the proposal stage (Bodilly et al., 1996; Bodilly, 1998). The literature indicates that these would have to be developed for the teams to be successful in implementing across many schools. Thus, it could be expected that teams would create more fully developed implementation strategies over time, especially ones that might address issues of teacher capacity or lack of funding.

In judging the effects of these types of adaptations, past policy analysts looked for strict adherence to the original policy or policy fidelity (Goggin et al., 1990). Given what we know of other implementations and the call for adaptability in designs, we would expect the designs to change. Fidelity to the original designs is, therefore, a way of gauging the changes but not really judging their importance or the nature of their effect on achieving the desired outcomes.

For the purposes of this document we propose an analytic scheme that accords with the original ideas of the RFP but does not require fidelity to individual components described in the original design documents. The problem statement explicit in the concept of the comprehensive design in the RFP was that current school organizations and education programs were fragmented, incoherent, and inconsistent. This led ultimately to poor student outcomes. The comprehensive design was to align the standards, assessments, curriculum, instruction, professional development, and governance components of a school and supporting policies into a comple-

---

traditions. The story of implementation of NAS designs will be the story of attempting to meet two possibly conflicting goals: being highly innovative and maintaining high quality versus being able to implement rapidly in many existing schools.

. . . The scale-up strategy NAS adopted can be considered complex. In terms of the implementation literature, this often means that many actors are involved and that these actors can have a strong influence on the progress of the initiative. Importantly, each often controls only a part of the decisionmaking process, leading to a "fragmented" policy environment. . . . In school literature, "complexities of joint action" often result in a phenomenon labeled "mutual adaptation" or "mutual adjustment," in which the implementation slows, and the intervention changes over time.

mentary whole that worked to produce a coherent and effective educational experience for students to enable improved student performance on multiple dimensions. The operative words are *coherent* and *complementary* components that would lead to a *comprehensive* whole. The designs in the end should still be coherent. If, as they adapt or as they are implemented, designs become incoherent with internally inconsistent components, then the policy concept of a design itself is brought into question.

One might argue that the incoherence of a design is irrelevant if, as a school attempts to adopt it, student performances improve. Improved performance, however, would not be attributable to the concept of a design as NAS has envisioned it. Certainly other factors, such as alternative curriculum programs adopted by the schools, would have to be ruled out as potential causes. But research now points to an interesting phenomenon: As intervenors in organizations attempt to ensure their intervention is accepted and implemented, they often develop strong support strategies or strong implementation strategies (Bikson and Eveland, 1998; Bikson et al., 1997; Bikson and Eveland, 1992; Eveland and Bikson, 1989), and it is these implementation strategies that actually cause the positive effect, not the adoption of the intervention. So for example, in a school adopting a design, it might never actually implement the design or only implement it poorly, but the infusion of funding and services and materials bought under the implementation program might serve teachers and students well. Increased professional development, improved technology, better materials in the classroom could all be part of the implementation support offered to a school adopting a design. Student performance might increase as a result of this, even if the school never actually adopted the standards, assessments, curriculum, or instructional strategies of the design.

HOW WE WENT ABOUT THE STUDY

Our methodology for this study is straightforward and simple. Over the course of the RAND relationship with NAS, we have collected various data. This particular analysis is based heavily on the following sources: a review of the original design documents; review of intervening and current documentation on the teams and their designs; interviews with the teams over the course of the entire period (we interviewed or interacted with design team personnel on many different occasions, perhaps 15 to 20 times for each team); and a review by design teams of the analysis.

Other data we have collected have shed light on the analysis. We have done extensive interviewing during the different phases of the effort (Bodilly et al., 1995; Bodilly et al., 1996; Bodilly, 1998). We interviewed district personnel involved in these efforts at least twice for each district, including approximately 18 districts in the demonstration phase and eight districts in the scale-up phase. We interviewed school personnel in these districts including personal interviews with over 70 principals (usually on two occasions a year apart). We interviewed approximately 750 teachers in group interviews during the course of these studies. These different data collection methods are summarized in Table 1.1. This report is based on a review of the documents and interview notes.

The documents reviewed were extensive, but three types of materials were most important. First, the original winning proposals submitted to NAS in February 1992 were reviewed and form the baseline for this analysis. Second, at key points NAS asked design teams to submit updated "Design Documents," for example, at the end of the development phase and at the end of the demonstration phase. Finally, most recently the design teams have submitted a range of materials that they currently use to introduce their designs to schools. These latter two sets of design documents were reviewed and contrasted with the first set.

To further ensure that the designs are now as we describe them, this document was reviewed by each of the teams and NAS for accuracy. Their revisions and suggestions were incorporated into the document as appropriate.

The document is historical in nature. In this review we try to capture our best sense of the changes that have occurred, the reasons behind those changes, and their significance, if any. It captures a period of time from 1991 to 1998. It is based on our research of NAS in eight jurisdictions. In this sense, the report can be seen as an informed observer's view of an unfolding developmental process. It does not represent the current status of the teams or of the designs.

Table 1.1

Data Types and Sources

| | Structured Interviews | | | | Archival | |
	In Person	Phone	Observations	Document	News Items	Statistical Data on Schools
NAS	√		√	√	√	√
National design team	√	√		√	√	√
Local design team representative	√					
District				√	√	√
Superintendent	√					
Coordinators	√	√				
Title I	√					
Budget	√					√
School			√a	√	√	√
Principals	√					
Facilitators	√					
Teacher group	√					
Lead teachers	√					
Classrooms			√			
Union	√					
State representatives	√b					

[a]Limited.
[b]When the state was the primary partner with NAS (Kentucky).

We provide one major caveat to our analysis. Our baseline is the original proposals provided by teams in a competitive process. Competitors often overpromise what they intend to accomplish simply to gain the contract or award. We call this overselling and it is common in the field. In our discussions with design teams, several indicated this was the case for them. Given this, some of the deviations we track from the original proposals could be viewed simply as the result of initial deliberate overselling by teams. Operationally speaking, there is no way for us to make adjustments for the amount of change due simply to overselling. In any event each design had the same incentives, so all design teams would be biased in the same direction and to the same extent to oversell. We therefore have read the proposals literally as the intended vision of each design team, but we note several instances where design teams specifically said they had oversold the designs.

ORGANIZATION OF THE REPORT

Our research showed that the changes discerned fell into three areas: changes to the portfolio of designs caused by NAS's own funding and philosophical growth, changes to the designs' theories of education caused by further planned development and changes to adaptation in response to local conditions, and changes to the implementation strategies of teams as they strove to meet the demands for scale-up. Some changes have multiple causes; therefore, disentangling cause and effect is and will remain problematic.

This report is organized around those three change areas. Chapter Two deals with the most obvious: changes to the portfolio of designs. Specifically three design teams were dropped and one was denied strong support for a period of several years. It is instructive to detail the reasons they were not granted further funding or did not participate in the NAS district scale-up strategy. Chapter Three describes the changes made to the designs themselves due to planned development, adaptation to the needs of the clients served, and accommodation to the districts in which the schools served were embedded. Chapter Four then describes the changes in implementation strategies of the teams as they sought to serve more sites and maintain some quality assurances. The final chapter presents our conclusions and discusses their implications for policymakers.

Chapter Two

CHANGES IN THE PORTFOLIO OF TEAMS AND NAS'S STRATEGY

As indicated in the literature, the concept of a whole-school design as epitomized by the team designs supported by NAS would depend greatly upon the fortunes and prerogatives of the major funder: NAS. At least some of the changes that have occurred in the concept of a comprehensive design have been caused by strategic policy decisions made by NAS itself rather than individual design teams interacting in different locales. NAS as the funder or sponsor of teams has chosen to promote some teams and has eliminated others from both its funding and "policy umbrella." This chapter describes changes in the design portfolio—the decrease in designs and teams from the original 11 chosen from the competition in 1992 to the remaining seven that continued into the NAS district scale-up phase in 1995.[1] It addresses the questions:

- Which designs and teams continued into the NAS district scale-up initiative and which did NAS no longer fund? Why?

- What does the portfolio of designs and teams still included say about the relative emphases of the NAS notion of design and design-based assistance?

Not much has been written in public documents about the reasons behind these reductions, but they are important and are different for the two phases in which they took place. This chapter covers the

---

[1]LALC was given more time to develop its design but did take part in the NAS district scale-up. It rejoined NAS in 1997 and began scale-up in the Los Angeles Basin.

changes made in the portfolio both when NAS moved from development into the demonstration phase and when NAS moved from demonstration to scale-up.

Much of the explanation revolves around NAS's original mission, which was not just to develop designs but to spread them. The RFP outlined seven questions that each proposal would have to answer. The seventh was:

> Explain how you will persuade others to put your design in place. . . . Bidders will be expected to demonstrate their understanding of the complexities of implementing their design, outline initial strategies for proceeding, and provide at least a general idea of how they plan to encourage adaptation and use of the design following initial testing and implementation. (NASDC, 1991, p. 25)

Three phases of development, shown in Figure 1.1, were outlined in the proposal: development, demonstration, and scale-up. The scale-up phase was simply designated as Phase 3 in the request for proposal, but teams were directed to pay attention to it. NAS required that one product from the development year would be a plan for Phase 3.

> The Phase 3 strategy and associated analysis should demonstrate that the design can be adopted or re-created by many communities, that the design team has thought through the difficulties likely to arise and how they can be solved, and how the design team plans to help many communities simultaneously to adapt, re-create and operate its design. (NASDC, 1991, p. 29)

The story of the noncontinuation of these designs and teams is in large part the story of whether teams understood and paid attention to this part of the mission of NAS.

REDUCTION PRIOR TO THE DEMONSTRATION PHASE

In 1992 11 teams were awarded contracts for a year of further specification and development of concepts. NAS intended that specification and development were to take at least three important forms.

First, in that year, teams were to work their original 50-page proposals into the full range of ideas and materials needed by schools and districts to understand and implement the designs. For example, depending on the specific design, the following would need to be developed and clearly specified:

- Content and performance standards for all students
- Curriculum and instructional packages either fully specified or in the form of guidelines for further specification by teachers
- Packages of information for districts and schools to use to set up the decentralized regulatory environment envisioned
- A set of assessments or assessment practices for teachers to access
- Guidelines on or models integrating health and social services into the school.

In short, the expected outcome of this phase was a full and rich set of materials describing for laymen and practitioners what they needed to do to set the design in motion in their schools or providing them with the actual materials to be used in the case of a prescribed curriculum. The teams were to move past rhetoric and provide the substantive materials for implementation.

Second, teams had provided very little in the way of implementation strategies in their original proposals. This time was to be used to develop implementation approaches and to outline plans for Phase 3. For example, teams were to specify: how schools would choose to align with a design; training regimes for teachers and principals; how schools would afford the design; and plans for the acquisition of needed materials and technology in schools.

Finally, NAS expected the teams to articulate how they intended to promote the goal of national diffusion of the designs and to indicate their ability to do so. NAS carefully warned teams that traditional means of presentation to research groups at national conferences were *not* what it had in mind.

By the end of the development year, NAS was experiencing funding difficulties (Glennan, 1998). Whether it would have significant funding to proceed through its full initiative as originally planned was uncertain, and NAS began to look for ways to reduce its funding commitment. The most obvious was to reduce the number of teams or to reduce the average amount given to teams. By the time of the decision to proceed to the demonstration phase, NAS had decided to cut teams, but what would be the basis for that decision?

NAS set out on fact-finding missions, sending teams of NAS staff, RAND staff, and members of the NAS Educational Advisory Committee to visit design teams and assess them according to criteria developed by NAS.[2] Notes from these missions were assembled and reviewed internally by NAS, and teams were provided opportunities to display, discuss, and present their progress verbally to NAS in extensive meetings. With these data, NAS made its decisions.

Two teams, Odyssey in North Carolina and Bensenville New American Schools Project in Illinois, could be characterized as having "district-based" designs. The proposals came from and were led by district personnel and focused on how those districts would reform themselves. Both proposals included ideas about break-the-mold schools, but they were centered on and particular to those districts' needs. Other design teams could be characterized as being external providers (not part of the governmental structure of local education) or as having a significant group of external providers leading the design.[3]

During the development year, both of these district-based teams became embroiled in local political battles that centered on the designs (Mirel, 1994; Mickelson and Wadsworth, 1996). In both cases the district initiatives had led to reactions by forces against some of the constructs of the designs or against the manner in which the

---

[2]NAS created a group of Educational Advisors to act in a consultative manner when called upon. These advisors included policy experts, principals, teachers, and professors.

[3]Los Angeles Learning Centers was also "district based," but with a difference. The district was one of several partners to the effort: The teachers union, a major not-for-profit reform group, and two universities were co-partners. The nonprofit evolved into the lead of the team. In this way the design was not tied exclusively to the dictates of the central office, rather it was an attempt by several groups to combine forces for reform.

district had tried to accomplish change.[4] For example, some teachers and parents accused the central office in Gaston, North Carolina, of not allowing them to participate in the creation of the design and not allowing opportunities to hear their views about some of the constructs of the design. NAS's fact-finding indicated that in both cases the districts had not effectively led the initiatives so as to build stakeholder support of the design, and it was clear that the design could not go forward given the level of political antagonism evident from important constituencies. NAS's review of materials indicated that the district staff time was being taken up in these political battles and not in the further specification and development of the design parameters.

After reading the proposals for development and diffusion by these two teams, NAS concluded that the districts did not understand NAS's intentions concerning scale-up or simply did not choose to follow that lead. The teams' scale-up proposals focused on presentations at conferences and mailing of materials about the district efforts and did not deal with how the design team would support implementation in other districts. In contrast, other teams talked of moving to schools throughout the country and of a strong implementation support system.

In June 1993 NAS dropped the two district-based teams and district-focused designs and proceeded with the nine teams and their designs that were not connected to specific districts or led exclusively by district personnel. NAS would no longer have teams whose ability to develop the design would rest so heavily on the team's ability to navigate the dangerous waters of local politics. In short, the lesson learned was that district-led designs were politically untenable and unscalable.

The impact on the portfolio was straightforward. NAS would not support design teams based inside a local central office, nor would it support designs that were not transferable to schools or districts around the country. NAS would support only design teams that were external to the local governance structure, and only those teams

---

[4]In one case, the unions became set against the design. In another, conservative religious groups were actively set against implementation of the design in their community.

serious about scale-up outside a "home" district or locality were acceptable.

REDUCTION AFTER THE DEMONSTRATION PHASE BEFORE GOING TO SCALE

The demonstration phase (July 1993 to July 1995) was to be used by teams to demonstrate that their concepts could be implemented in real schools and to work with schools to adapt the designs as needed for scale-up. A considerable grant from the Annenberg Foundation relieved some of NAS's budget constraints. In addition, the design teams were to submit business plans for expansion and scale-up at the end of this period by which NAS would judge their readiness to proceed.

NAS had a business-oriented board that wanted to bring more business-like practices to schools; it emphasized the ability of teams to show performance and financial independence. In keeping with its business philosophy, the board made clear to the NAS staff that it was not interested, and never had been, in promoting a group of financially dependent organizations, and it insisted that the scale-up phase include a move to fee-for-service by the teams. Thus, the NAS staff was encouraged to use its best judgments to remove teams that could not show an ability to deliver on the promises of the design, that had a limited potential market within the United States, or that could not show an ability to become financially independent from NAS.

NAS again set up a fact-finding team. The fact-finding team included NAS staff and members of the NAS Educational Advisory Committee. In addition, RAND reports on progress were used to assess each team's situation. At this time, RAND reported that the teams showed a great deal of variation in approach, stability, and ability to scale up (Bodilly et al., 1996). Four teams appeared to be able to implement their designs, while four were having more difficulty. In addition, NAS staff's review of the business plans submitted by the teams indicated that several teams were not taking the switch to fee-for-service seriously. Several also did not address the issue of scale-up in a manner deemed acceptable by NAS.

CLC was identified as facing serious implementation challenges and also appeared to be reluctant to expand in a manner that NAS deemed acceptable. CLC had always been closely aligned with the charter school movement in Minnesota and wished to expand, at least for the time being, only within the confines of Minnesota under the charter school laws of that state. From NAS's point of view the charter school focus limited the market of CLC, as did the state-based focus.

LALC was identified as being relatively behind in its development. At this time, LALC was experiencing a leadership turnover and had not completed its design work. It was in a situation similar to the two district-based designs dropped earlier. With strong ties to the central office and union, which were partners to the effort, it was focused on solving the educational problems in the Los Angeles school district. Its design development had suffered from the difficulties involved in building a collaborative effort among partners driven by local political concerns, and LALC could not commit to a scale-up strategy outside Los Angeles for several years, until it completed its design work. Later, it planned to remain within the southern California area or near Western states. By committing to this limited geographical area the LALC design team argued it could potentially reach a significant percentage of the school-age population of the United States and serve its target population of urban schools.

In July 1995, NAS removed CLC from its portfolio; it provided funding to LALC to complete its development but did not invite it to be part of the NAS scale-up strategy. NAS offered to reconsider later whether LALC was ready to join the NAS scale-up initiative. Neither team would be part of the scale-up movement into partner jurisdictions in Fall 1995. De facto this removed the last of the district-associated teams from the portfolio (LALC) as well as one associated with the laws of a particular state (CLC).

As a final footnote to this progression, LALC continued its own development, eventually transforming itself into the Urban Learning Centers (ULC). It further developed its materials through strong stable leadership and began to expand to districts within the Los Angeles Basin. ULC continued to attend NAS conferences and meetings, and in 1997 NAS decided the team was ready for full participation in scale-up. ULC is now considered a fully participating NAS team.

Since LALC/ULC did not take part in NAS's district scale-up strategy and did not expand outside its original jurisdictions until recently, we do not include the design in the remainder of this report.

NEW STRATEGY FOR SCALE-UP

In the Introduction we gave some information about the scale-up strategy. Here we explain the implications for these portfolio decisions. At the same time as these decisions were being made, two other important decisions were made at NAS.

First, the NAS leadership turned over for the third time. John Anderson, formerly of IBM and the Business Roundtable, became president of NAS, and his thinking seriously guided the scale-up strategy. Anderson, through his own experiences and knowledge of others, was convinced that districts and states had to provide a supportive environment or the design concept would not flourish. This view was bolstered by a RAND report on the demonstration phase that indicated that demonstration sites were having difficulties implementing the designs because of conflicting district policies or lack of support (Bodilly et al., 1996).

The concept of a supportive environment as developed by NAS included school-level autonomy on budget, staffing, and curriculum and instruction; high standards that matched those of both the designs and assessments; significant sources of professional development funding and technology; systemic support for community services at the school level; and public engagement in educational reform (Bodilly, 1998; New American Schools, 1995). These concepts had considerable overlap with the NARE district-level strategy.[5] Indeed NARE and its advocates had heavily influenced Anderson and NAS in their thinking.

---

[5]While NAS rejected the district-led teams, it did not reject the need for a strongly supportive district environment. The NARE team was not district led but was an organization external to the school systems in which it worked like the other remaining teams. However, unlike the other teams, NARE had developed state and district concepts for a supportive environment.

Second, as indicated in the Introduction, NAS decided on a strategy of scale-up in a limited number of districts.[6] It imposed four ideas on design teams: (1) teams would have to work in districts that NAS chose and that were presumably supportive of the design concept; (2) NAS would oversee the process of choosing those districts and guiding the initial school selection process; (3) multiple designs would work within a single district; and (4) the teams would charge fees for design-based assistance. Not only would schools "buy" the design, they would buy the services of the teams to help them implement the designs (design-based assistance).

This jurisdiction strategy had two different parts: the NAS jurisdiction strategy and the NARE jurisdiction strategy. NAS, representing the seven teams, entered into negotiations with six jurisdictions: Cincinnati, Dade, Maryland, Memphis, Philadelphia, and San Antonio.

In contrast, NARE—during its conception, development, and demonstration phases—had already entered into agreements with several different jurisdictions. NARE believed that individual schools could not implement and sustain design concepts by themselves and that schools needed a network of other schools and districts working together to sustain changes. Given this district-level approach, NARE developed partnerships with several districts and states including Arkansas, Vermont, New York, Rochester NY, White Plains NY, San Diego CA, Pittsburgh PA, Kentucky, and Washington state. These partnerships predated the NAS jurisdiction strategy and in fact were the philosophical basis for the NAS jurisdiction strategy. These NARE jurisdictions already had multiple schools implementing the NARE design in 1995.

NAS worked with several of these original NARE jurisdictions, in concert with NARE, to make them NAS partners as well, including San Diego, Pittsburgh, Kentucky, and Washington state. But for the most part these NARE jurisdictions did not quickly accept non-NARE designs into their jurisdictions. By 1998, the other NAS designs had made no headway in the NARE jurisdictions with the exception of a few demonstration schools in San Diego and a few schools in

---

[6]Recall that design teams were also free to partner with schools outside the NAS selected districts.

Washington state. Likewise, NARE had not made headway into the new NAS districts. In keeping with its regional philosophy, NARE did not actively pursue schools in the other NAS districts because they lacked commitment to the NARE district philosophy.

Thus, while NAS claims to have worked with ten different jurisdictions, in fact several were primarily NARE jurisdictions and had no more than two to five non-NARE schools using designs from the other teams. This will become important in Chapter Three in explaining the different changes made to designs.

As discussed by Glennan (1998), NAS's choice of districts was less than ideal. Rather than obtaining partnerships with districts with highly supportive environments, NAS soon found that it had partnered with primarily urban districts with very challenged student populations. More important, these districts, despite their rhetoric, had not in large part adopted the reform strategy outlined by NAS as supportive of comprehensive school designs. To remedy this situation, NAS promised the teams it would work with the districts to build a supportive environment. It proposed to aid, in some unspecified ways, partnering districts to provide more coherent and cohesive support for design-based schools (Glennan, 1998).[7]

This new strategy and role combined with the portfolio reduction to produce the following strategy of complex interactions necessary for success:

- Design teams would provide designs and assistance to schools.

- NAS would market the designs to a set of districts that either had or were willing to work toward supportive environments.

- Districts would work to become more supportive of designs and design-based assistance.

- Jointly, teams, NAS, and districts would develop a new system of education supportive of designs and improved student performance.

---

[7]As the years have gone by, NAS has aided districts in different ways; in particular, it has published a series of "how to" papers by various consultants offering guidance.

SUMMARY AND IMPLICATIONS OF NAS PORTFOLIO AND STRATEGY CHANGES

Funding concerns drove the reduction in number of design teams and designs.   These changes can be seen as unplanned and necessitated by unpredictable events that overtook the funder and, therefore, the teams.   In addition, three teams suffered from unplanned, slow design development connected to political problems due to the teams' base in local governance.   This base magnified the negative effects on their designs of leadership turnover and inability to develop stakeholder support.   Given these funding and political concerns, NAS chose to eliminate design teams and designs that did not suit its philosophy of reform.   NAS made choices to exclude certain types of design teams and design concepts and to include others.

The portfolio changes reveal a specific concept of a design that had taken hold at NAS by 1995. The remaining teams had common characteristics in terms of a portfolio:

- Groups external to local educational governmental structures, including schools, led the teams. Local political bodies could not make effective design teams because of their inability to rise above local political situations and the need for stakeholder buy-in. Homegrown, school-based designs and homegrown, district-based initiatives were thought to be less effective or compelling approaches to reform.

- Connected to this, the school was seen as the target of intervention that the design teams and their designs would be able to influence most readily. A school-level design was thought to be an essential ingredient to a larger reform strategy. Thus, all designs had to have a school-level focus. This did not preclude teams from having district or state designs and implementation strategies, but they all had to minimally have a school design and strategy.

- The designs were no longer focused on a local area's problems. They were not associated strongly or exclusively with a particular locality, population, or state but had "national" appeal. In a sense, this implies that to be adaptable to local circumstances the designs had to be generic and not focused on a single locale's circumstances.

- Schools and districts would be willing to pay for effective, externally developed designs, and design teams would operate and implement their designs in a competitive, fee-for-service market.

- The design concept could not be effective without district-level reform or a preexisting supportive environment. NAS took on the role of ensuring that systemic reform efforts moved forward in the partnering districts. Thus, at least in the partnering jurisdictions, the success of the teams and their designs were now dependent on the joint action of themselves, NAS, and the multiple players in the partner jurisdictions.

Only teams dedicated to these principles with designs that were consonant with these notions remained with NAS through the three-year scale-up period. NAS continued its push to get large numbers of implementing schools in these districts. To do so it had to become more "market sensitive" or sensitive to the needs of these unreformed, but reforming, districts.

This chain of events indicated a growing understanding by NAS of the difficulties of school reform and how it had to be embedded in larger reforms. But the increased number of players in the strategy and their respective roles increased the complexity involved, increased the interdependence of the different groups, and raised the probability of strong effects from political factors, joint actions, and mutual adjustments.

Chapter Three

CHANGES TO THE THEORY OF EDUCATION INHERENT IN THE DESIGNS

This chapter covers the changes to the theory of education behind the designs that went into the scale-up phase—AC, ATLAS, CON, ELOB, MRSH, NARE, and RW. Specifically, it addresses those components of the designs that were the main focus of the RFP and through content analysis were the main focus of the design: standards and assessments, curriculum, instruction, governance, community involvement, and professional development (Bodilly et al., 1995). These are not all the components, nor is every facet covered. By covering these major elements of the designs we hope to convey the nature of the changes made and the reasons for those changes.

The Introduction noted several ways in which the designs themselves might be expected to change and adapt. In this chapter we try to draw some distinctions among these different manners or types of change. The distinctions that were most evident, but not always clearly disentangled from one another, are planned development, gradual adaptation to meet student needs or to reduce conflict with existing policy, and reconceptualization.

Planned development. Each of the designs moved from initial low levels of specification to higher levels of specification. For example, several designs started out with just ideas about project-based curriculum. These designs, through the help of teachers in the field, developed many units of curriculum.

Gradual adaptation to meet specific student or teacher (client) needs. NAS scale-up strategy and the districts it chose to work with pushed the design teams into largely urban, high-poverty, largely minority, low-achieving schools for at least two reasons. These districts were most interested in improving student performance and had the most to gain by doing so, and these districts tended to have large allotments of federal Title I funds that could be applied to such efforts. The districts serving these populations tended to demand basic skills curriculum and instruction programs from the teams, regardless of the design. At the demand of the districts, teams often gradually adapted their designs to meet the needs of these students. In addition, teams found that teachers in these districts had needs different from what was originally thought in their proposals or lacked capacity to implement the design without more significant supports. Some new features were developed in response to these teacher needs.

Gradual adaptation due to conflict with existing policy set. Initially NAS assumed that the partner districts it chose for scale-up were supportive of the "whole-school design" philosophy. NAS soon found that the districts had policies, rules, and regulations that conflicted with the NAS philosophy and strategy. Interactions among these actors and their policies often resulted in gradual design adaptation.

Reconceptualization. When a design team discovers that in the real world certain elements of its design conflict with one another or simply do not add to the efficacy of the design, it then rethinks the design and removes or adjusts one of the elements. We labeled this *reconceptualization.*

Throughout this chapter, aside from the tables, little mention is made of NARE. NARE's experience was significantly different from that of the other teams and stands as a counterexample. Most teams made progress on their planned developments and they also slowly made adaptations to their designs, but NARE refused to make adaptations along the way. Then after a period of considerable learning, NARE completely overhauled its design. In 1997–1998, after significant experience in the field, NARE retired its design and presented to the public a completely new design called America's Choice. It no longer supports the original NARE design; the design team considers the NARE design no longer functional. Meanwhile schools have now adopted the America's Choice design. We cover this experience in a separate section at the end of this chapter. In the tables in this chapter we tried to distinguish this manner of change in contrast to the gradual adaptations made by other designs, and we designated this as reconceptualization as well.

STANDARDS

NAS was created in the midst of a hot debate on national standards and the creation of panels to develop such standards.[1] Proponents argued strongly that a single set of curriculum standards, similar to those used in European countries, was needed, while others argued against this. At the same time professional societies were at work creating their own curriculum standards, and several research groups were also inventing standards (Gandal, 1996; University of Pittsburgh, 1992; National Center for History in the Schools, 1996; National Science Teachers Association, 1993; National Council of Teachers of Mathematics, 1989).

Part of the debate focused on performance and content standards. Many states and districts had content standards that dictated the coverage of specific content by grade level. For example, a content standard might specify that the events leading up to the Mayflower Compact would be covered in the fourth grade. But few states or districts had performance standards that explicitly detailed the types of work or products that students should be able to produce.

Another part of the debate was closely related and focused on the need for students to learn and demonstrate higher-order thinking skills and work-life skills. Rather than being able to recite the date of the Mayflower Compact, this school of thought insisted that the students should be able to explain the importance of it in the context of American history. When aligned with performance standards, a student might be required to have written a paper on the issue that required some research. The paper would have to demonstrate mastery of the subject, put the subject into context, and pass muster on grammatical correctness.

---

[1] In 1990 Congress established the National Education Goals Panel and in 1991 it established the National Council on Education Standards and Testing to address the issue of national standards.

Standards in the Original Proposals

The teams' original proposals reflected that time period when few models for standards existed. The original proposals contained different approaches to the development of standards and assessment packages with one exception. All designs noted that standards were the starting point of designs and that standards needed to be aligned with design assessments, curriculum, and instruction. Teams intended that their standards be adopted in all their schools to guide the coherence of the curriculum and instruction and set the mission of the school in motion.

While they all agreed with this fundamental principle, significant differences existed in the proposals.

- **All teams adopted high standards for all students.**

- **Two teams adopted an existing set of standards and assessments.** ELOB adopted the International Baccalaureate standards for its schools as well as the Outward Bound principles. RW in partnership with the State of Maryland adopted the new Maryland standards and the Maryland School Performance Assessment Program (MSPAP).

- **AC, MRSH, and NARE adapted national professional standards into a design team unique set.** For each of these teams, all schools were expected to adopt these standards. For example, MRSH mixed standards from the different national professional societies with work skills and higher-order thinking skills to create its own unique blend of standards at the elementary level. At the high school level MRSH adopted the Advanced Placement standards, but all MRSH schools were expected to use these MRSH standards. NARE worked with experts at the University of Pittsburgh's Learning Research and Development Center (LRDC) on the New Standards Project, a well-funded attempt to develop high-quality content and performance standards in all subjects.

- **CON and ATLAS blended national standards with local interest to develop a unique set of standards for each site.** The two teams proposed that with the aid of the team each school would develop a unique set of standards. The CON design emphasized the use of national professional societies' standards, but with adaptation to local circumstances and interests. ATLAS was less definitive: "Each school community will commit itself to working out high standards of student achievement within and across the conventional disciplines, as well as to other valued areas such as the arts. These standards will be articulated through intensive and extensive discussions among all stakeholders." (ATLAS Proposal, 1992, p. 28.)

Intervening Experiences

In the years following the initial award of contracts, different professional societies put forward new standards that achieved wide acceptance—math, English, and geography (University of Pittsburgh, 1992). Others failed to do so; for example, the history standards were universally criticized, apparently pleasing no one (Gandal, 1995, 1996).

At the same time, rather than accept a single national set, even if it was voluntary, states and districts began to develop their own sets of standards. They were encouraged in this regard by federal grants under the Goals 2000 program directed at state endeavors to bring all children to high standards, and states could use this money to fund standards development. The early 1990s saw a rejuvenation of local efforts to develop high standards for all students. Many districts and several states created collaborative teams to develop unique sets of standards that included content and skill areas and in some cases even performance standards. This was aided by efforts such as the New Standards project and the 1994 reauthorization of Title I that pushed states in this direction. As of 1996, 48 states were developing new academic content standards (Gandal, 1996).

Meanwhile, those design teams that had proposed the development of their own standards attempted to do so. NARE continued its development of standards through its participation in the New Standards Project with the University of Pittsburgh and others. MRSH in particular spent considerable resources in the development of a standards and assessment package. Very early on, one team had an immediate setback on standards: ELOB realized that the International Baccalaureate standards conflicted with the Outward Bound principles and with the instructional approach of extensive project-based learning proposed. By 1994 ELOB had dropped the International Baccalaureate standards and began a development phase of its own.

By Fall 1995 the scale-up phase brought a new reality concerning standards to the design teams and NAS. NAS thought that schools accepting a design would accept the content standards that went with those designs, which also implied acceptance of a curriculum and assessment package matched to design team standards. The harsh reality was that districts and states, having taken the extensive trouble to develop new standards and gain widespread agreement on them, were not willing to put aside their standards in favor of different sets for each design team working in the district. State content standards could not be put aside in any case as they were mandatory.

Discussions between NAS, design teams, districts, and schools focused intensely on this issue for the first two years of the scale-up phase. Over that time period a loose protocol began to develop. Before agreeing to work with a particular design team, the district would demand to see a "cross-walk," as it became known, between the design team standards and its own. In a cross-walk, design teams reviewed their standards against the district's and showed how the design team standard either met or exceeded the district's standards.

The results of cross-walks of district or state standards to design standards had varying results. For example, Ohio has state standards that are incorporated into the Ohio State Proficiency Exams that every student must pass and that dictate the scope and sequence of the curriculum throughout the state. Cincinnati found favor with the Roots and Wings reading component Success for All, but not with the science/social studies component of the design. Thus, Success for All was approved for implementation, but not World Lab. The governor of the state of Wisconsin endorsed the MRSH standards for use throughout the state, but Cincinnati saw lapses in it in terms of multiculturalism and would not allow MRSH to operate in that city. Meanwhile, Memphis City Public Schools in Tennessee allowed all designs to operate in its schools.

Standards as of 1998

The changes evident in the standards are not unique to particular designs but rather a trend across all of them. In an example of planned development, most teams continued to develop their own standards prior to the scale-up phase. The scale-up phase brought a different response. In an example of gradual adaptation to conflicting district policies, the teams evolved away from the insistence that their design standards be adopted as the sole standards for the partnering schools. In a compromise with districts, teams including NARE have developed the cross-walking process. In the NAS and NARE districts, every design team meets the district standards or does not work in that district. Schools can use the team's standard only if there is no conflict and it is a higher standard. Thus, the designs have changed from having their own unique standards to using the district standards and meeting districts' requirements. NARE, however, still promotes its standards and assessment package in districts using its "district strategy."

After several years of experience with districts and their content standards packages, the designs have evolved in the following ways, as shown in Table 3.1.

- Some teams adapted national professional standards into a design team unique set. Four teams (AC, CON, MRSH, NARE) reviewed different national standards and adapted them into a set unique for each of their respective designs. For each of these teams, schools are expected to adopt these content standards, with one major caveat; see next bullet.

- Some teams use existing district content standards. Most teams have content standards for all students but agree to meet or abide by the district content standards in each district in which they work, using a cross-walk process to determine a good match. Design team standards can and often do exceed the district standards, in which case the schools can adopt the design team standard. For example, AC standards include significant work-related skills and specific types of performances that are added onto existing district standards. CON still encourages some modest local school additions to standards (no longer adaptations).

Table 3.1

Standards Changes

Team	Proposal 1992	Design Materials 1998	Reason for Change
AC	• Adopt existing sets of national standards to create design-unique set used by each school	• Further develop own standards • Use district standards and supplement with design standards	• Planned development • Adapt to conflicting district standards
ATLAS	• Each school uses constructivist approach to create locally unique set based on design principles	• Use district standards and supplement with design principles	• Adapt to conflicting district standards
CON	• Adapt existing sets of standards to create design-specific set • Allow local supplementation and adaptation	• Further develop own standards • Use district standards and supplement with design standards	• Planned development • Adapt to conflicting district standards
ELOB	• Adopt International Baccalaureate standards and Outward Bound design principles	• Drop International Baccalaureate standards • Develop principles • Use district standards and supplement with design principles	• Reconceptualization • Planned development • Adapt to conflicting district standards
MRSH	• Adopt existing or develop own	• Fully develop own standards • Use district standards and supplement with design standards	• Planned development • Adapt to conflicting district standards
NARE	• Significantly adapt national standards to create design-unique set called New Standards	• Fully develop NARE standards • Promote use of design standards • Permit use of district standards, but only after review of design standards	• Planned development • Reconceptualization
RW	• Adopt Maryland state standards for demonstration schools	• Use district standards and supplement with design standards	• Adapt to conflicting district standards

- Some teams base the standards in design principles. Two teams, ELOB and ATLAS, have adopted a principle-based approach. Design principles are used as the basis for all activities within the schools, and standards are no exception. A school will still accept and meet district standards, but the school must also adopt the principles of the design. As an example, ELOB principles include the use of reflection, self-assessment, and learning from mistakes, which can be translated into a teacher peer review process, students drafting and redrafting their work, and students reflecting on their work against a given set of performance standards in order to improve it toward a higher standard. These principles represent a different type of standard for the school. For ATLAS, the community of stakeholders is responsible for developing standards that support the five principles of the ATLAS design.[2]

The major implication of this evolution is that even within a design, schools using the design will adopt different standards depending on the local circumstances. These standards might not match the assessments, curriculum, or instruction packages proposed by the team.

ASSESSMENTS

At the time of the proposals some part of the debate in the larger educational community circled around the issue of valid testing, with many groups calling for more authentic assessments and movement away from standardized testing regimes with their heavy reliance on multiple-choice items. If indeed students should have higher-order thinking skills and be able to perform complex analytic tasks, then these ideas should be incorporated into assessments. In short there was, and still is, concern that the assessments used did not reflect the knowledge children were to acquire. And if inappropriate assessments were used, curriculum and instruction would soon

---

[2]ATLAS does not have a given set of standards. It has kept with its original concept of locally developed or at least approved standards. "In ATLAS communities, standards are based on what the people closest to the students think is important for their students to know" (ATLAS Communities, 1995, p. 7).

follow suit, with teachers enforcing skill and drill routines to prepare students for rote memorization types of tests.

Assessments in the Original Proposals

Design teams were not immune to this call for more authentic assessments matched to the high standards being developed. In their original proposals, all demanded more authentic assessments including performance-based assessments (in which students are asked to perform tasks that demonstrate their learning or must create the responses themselves as opposed to tests that ask for students to choose between already constructed answers) that were aligned with their standards. The particulars of the proposals varied:

- **All teams encouraged performance assessments.** The designs as a group encouraged and developed performance expectations as part of the standards setting process. Consonant with this they argued for performance-based assessments.

- **Some teams required specific project completions for graduation to the next level.** For example, students in AC schools were to develop and implement constructive actions each semester as a culminating curricular event for passing to the next grade. In the high school grades these actions took the form of internships needed for graduation. Similarly, ELOB students would show mastery-level work on a series of project-based activities over the course of their school careers. Similar, but unique, performance standards applied in ATLAS and MRSH schools.

- **All hinted at the need for portfolios of student work.** Each team required the development of student portfolios as a way to encourage and track student work.

- **Some offered multiple alternatives to standardized tests.** ATLAS, CON, and MRSH sought to develop multiple types of assessment that would be relevant to the particular task the student was learning. They sought to involve teachers in a process of learning which types of assessments were appropriate and when.

- **Some teams developed tests to meet their standards or for individual student diagnosis.** RW developed its own set of assessments to be used internally for assessing student progress every eight to nine weeks and to be used to place students in appropriate groupings. MRSH developed a set of assessments for progressing from one grade cluster to the next. CON developed a bank of test questions that could be used by CON schools to develop on-the-spot, unique tests.

- **Some called for Individual Education Compacts (IEC)/Individual Education Plans (IEP).** CON, ELOB, and MRSH teams required the use of IEC or similar instruments to set individually tailored goals for students and to gauge each student's progress. The IEC idea is covered here because these teams tied the notion of an IEC to a student portfolio and a series of tests or projects that had to be completed for promotion to the next grade. RW also called for a series of assessments and portfolios and, like CON and MRSH, thought that these systems would be computer-based. The RW idea was not an IEC reviewed by parents and teachers and dictating a specific pathway for each student but was a placement/portfolio system.

Intervening Experiences

Entry into the scale-up phase again brought a harsh reality home. In the intervening years several states and districts had embraced high-stakes testing regimes. Even if these tests were more performance-based (had fewer multiple-choice, standardized elements) than state tests in the past, the tests were now being connected to accountability systems for schools, principals, teachers, and students. Student continuation and graduation often depended upon a student's test scores. For example, scores on the Ohio State Proficiency Exams determined whether a student attended summer school and whether he or she could graduate. In addition, in some states schools were evaluated based upon school-level test scores. The states of Kentucky, Maryland, Texas, Tennessee, and Florida, where NAS had district partnerships, had mandated tests that were used to put schools on "probation" lists.[3] Several states including Texas and Tennessee were going further by evaluating principals and teachers based on the test scores produced by students in their schools and classes.

These testing regimes had a greater impact on the design teams than they might have otherwise because of the particular schools in which they began to work. As indicated in Chapter One, the schools that NAS designs worked in with partner jurisdictions tended to be high-poverty, high-minority, low-achieving schools. A significant number were on probation lists or close to it. Dade, San Antonio, and Memphis were identified by their respective states as having the lowest-performing schools in the state, and the districts were put on notice to improve. Specific schools were singled out as in need of improvement or put on probation. In the districts' attempts to meet increasing demands for test score improvements, they turned to NAS with the expectation that designs would improve scores on these tests, and they were not strongly interested in whether scores improved on more authentic assessments developed by the design teams.

In RAND's three years of work in these districts and schools, the power of high-stakes tests became more evident. As teams have attempted to institute performance-based assessments or more authentic assessments, they have met head on the teachers' felt need to ensure student performance on state or district tests. Significant periods of the school year are devoted to exercises to do well on these tests, regardless of the design. Thus, while teams have made efforts to develop more authentic assessment practices, these often have been pushed to the lowest levels—individual teachers' practices at the teacher's discretion. Schools and teachers still use district assessment practices by and large. Design team assessment

_____

[3]Implications for being on a probation list differ from place to place. Being put on probation often means the school is put on notice that it must improve its performance on state-mandated exams within three years or face "takeover" by the state. In Kentucky the state intervenes by providing a master educator to the site to help the site diagnose its problems and to provide on-site professional development. In other states, the threat of takeover is real but undefined. San Antonio and the state of Maryland have actually reconstituted schools—shutting the school doors, hiring new staff, and assigning new students.

practices might be added to, but do not substitute for, district assessment practices.

Meanwhile the adoption of IECs also came into conflict with existing practices and constraints.   IECs are expensive to develop and maintain, especially considering teachers' limited time.   As a practical matter few schools had the time resources to undertake implementation of the design and the professional development it entails, as well as to develop the detailed IEC for each student originally envisioned by designs such as CON, ELOB, or MRSH. MRSH sought to reduce this burden by the use of computer-based management tools, but schools did not have the resources to buy the computer packages or the time resources for all the data entry needed.   Thus, while the design still contains this element, the practicality is that the adoption of IECs is often the last item to be implemented, if implemented at all.

Design teams further developed and implemented an important practice—the development of rubrics matched to district standards. Early design documents did not address this explicitly—CON and ELOB were perhaps the exceptions.   Given that existing state standards could not be substituted, design teams were faced with a different issue: How could teachers be helped to develop curriculum to meet those standards and how could they help teachers uniformly and consistently grade students work against those standards? As early as 1994 these schools relayed this need to design teams. Over the intervening years several design teams have worked diligently to meet this need.

Assessments as of 1998

In an example of planned development, the teams progressed for some time in further developing their own assessments. However, new assessments were not demanded by schools and districts and in some ways were prohibited; thus, further development slowed in response to this low demand. The design teams have by and large not developed their own unique school-level assessments further. In an example of gradual adaptation to conflicting district policies, the designs no longer require the use of their school-level tests as replacements for district-mandated tests. Most agree with the use of district assessments as acceptable, if not totally valid, indicators.

Instead, design documents still call for more authentic assessments at the classroom level. The designs encourage more authentic practices within the school that might grow over time. Design team materials and assistance provide the means for teachers to develop classroom-based authentic assessments. While still not fully developed, all designs use portfolios as an important means to understand and assess student progress and track it over the stay of the student at the school.

Several quotes from MRSH help illustrate the transition that was made from original proposal to current practice. The original proposal called for the development of Hudson units—a new unit of measure replacing the Carnegie unit.

> The Hudson unit will be an output measurement. It will be used throughout our schools as the basic gauge of subject mastery. (MRSH Proposal, 1992, p. 23)

> At least three times per year assessments will be given to gauge mastery of the curriculum in each of the three instructional divisions. These watershed assessments, called external or exit exams in some locales, will measure accomplishment in each of the five core subjects. . . . We envision these new tests going well beyond the multiple choice varieties of the past and probably beyond paper and pencil technology. Exams at Hudson Schools will be the best, most comprehensive available. (p. 24)

The design now describes what it does as:

> The MRSH technical assistance helps participating schools compare student performance against the expectations established by their state as well as MRSH standards. . . . Assessing student progress is not limited to standardized tests, but also involves continued evaluation of student progress in meeting the educational needs of the school. Only then can teachers adjust and calibrate instruction to enable students to achieve high academic goals. (Modern Red Schoolhouse Institute leaflet, "Essential Elements," printed Nashville, TN)

The shift is away from the requirement of adoption of Hudson standards and assessments and toward working with district standards and providing additional, but not required, assessments other than the single standardized test mandated by the district.

Practices, such as the development of the IECs, that proved to be burdensome to schools have also been relegated to "advised" but not required.

Finally, in an example of adaptation to teacher needs, design teams further developed and implemented an important practice—the development of rubrics matched to district standards. AC, ATLAS, CON, ELOB, and MRSH all have developed processes as part of their designs to enable teachers to better understand the existing standards, to develop and embed them in the curriculum, and to work as a school or as grade-level teams to develop specific and consistent rubrics for grading.[4] RW has not progressed down this path primarily because it provides a standards-based curriculum to the school with specific classroom assessments embedded.

In summary, the assessment notions of the designs have been adapted to meet local circumstances largely because of conflicting state and district policies. But, in addition, previously unrealized needs of teachers have prompted the teams to develop rubrics that had not been a major emphasis of the original designs. The major implication is that schools using a single design will adopt different school-level assessments depending on the local circumstances. And, these assessments might not match the design's standards, curriculum, or instruction package.

CURRICULUM AND INSTRUCTION ELEMENTS

The designs varied significantly in their original proposals concerning curriculum and instruction. In this section we look at classroom instructional strategies, and in the next we focus on the use of student grouping for instruction.

---

[4]As an example, ELOB's *Guide for Planning a Learning Expedition* shows how to embed rubrics into the expedition use by students and teachers. Learning goals, standards, and a final assessment are part of each learning expedition plan and documentation. Displays of products from these expeditions viewed in Memphis show students detailing the goals and rubrics as an important initial step in the expeditionary process.

Table 3.2

Assessments Changes

Team	Proposal 1992	Design Materials 1998	Reason for Change
AC	• Portfolios • Required constructive actions	• Schools take district assessments and are judged by results	• Adapt to district assessment
ATLAS	• Authentic assessments • Portfolios • Performance requirements/exhibitions • Multiple alternative assessments keyed to tasks • Student teacher conf.	• Schools take district assessments and are judged by results • Added school rubrics • Student teacher conference	• Adapt to district assessment • Adapt to teacher needs • Planned development
CON	• Portfolios • Project completions • Design-specific assessment battery • IEP • Student/teacher/parent conferences	• Dropped: required design-specific battery, IEP, conferences • Schools take district assessments and are judged by results • Added school rubrics and class-level authentic assessments	• Adapt to district assessment • Adapt to teacher needs
ELOB	• Performance assessments • Portfolios • Requirements on expeditions • No standardized testing • IEP • Student/teacher/parent conferences	• Dropped: no standardized tests, IEP, conferences • Schools take district assessment and are judged by results • Review of student work	• Adapt to district assessment • Planned development
MRSH	• Required performances • Design specific assessment system • IEP	• Assessment system developed • De-emphasize MRSH assessment system—integrate into school's curriculum • De-emphasize IEP • Schools take district assessments and are judged by results	• Planned development • Adapt to district assessment
NARE	• Requires district and schools to adopt design-team developed assessments tied to New Standards	• Offers, but does not require, examinations provided by team aligned with New Standards and design team curriculum • Certification of Mastery • Portfolio system used	• Planned development • Reconceptualization
RW	• Use MSPAP in demonstration sites • Unique design-team diagnostic tests • Portfolios	• Schools take district test and are judged by results • Schools use RW assessments for diagnostics and internal placement • Portfolio system used	• Adapt to district assessment • Planned development

Curriculum and Instruction in the Original Proposals

In the original proposals, the designs held different philosophical and practical positions on the nature of curriculum and instruction, who would develop it, and how amenable it would be to flexible approaches given student interests and needs.   First, some teams emphasized curriculum and instructional strategies developed by the local sites, while others emphasized strategies developed solely by the design team.   Second, some design teams emphasized a student-driven approach with significant student choice of topics and delivery, while others emphasized a teacher-driven or design-driven approach.   Several designs appeared to favor progressive approaches to curriculum and instruction, while others favored more traditional approaches.

The RW design was at one end of the spectrum. The RW team position, as revealed in interviews and subsequent documents, was based on these premises:

- Most teachers did not have training in curriculum development and did not have the expertise to develop it. Nevertheless, most states and districts did not provide a rich and challenging curriculum package for teachers to use.

- Teachers had limited time during the school day and could not reasonably be held responsible for the development of curriculum within that time period.

- Many teachers used inappropriate instructional practices for particular tasks because they had not been trained to do otherwise, especially with at-risk children.

- Inappropriate instructional practices led to many students receiving poorly planned and executed curricular units and rote skill and drill instruction.

- Experts were needed to develop a firm curriculum and instructional approach for different learning tasks for teachers to use in classrooms.

Thus, RW promised to deliver a full set of curriculum and instructional materials closely matched to the Maryland standards. The curriculum and instruction would be standards-driven in this sense. The design team would be responsible for development of 1,600-plus hours of classroom teaching for grades K–5. Furthermore, or as a direct consequence of this position, the curriculum would be developmentally appropriate—the instructional strategies would fit the child's learning style at that stage in his or her life. Student choice was not a strong part of this design; neither, however, was teacher choice. While the teacher, not the student, provided the curriculum, in reality the design was intended to provide the full curriculum set and teachers would adopt it as their own.

The ELOB design provided the greatest contrast to this approach. The following positions demonstrate the difference:

- Teachers needed to develop their own curriculum and instruction as part of their professional development. Without having gone through this process and understanding it in detail, teachers could not become true professionals.

- Students had to take responsibility for their own learning. The team thought that students learn best when their creativity and curiosity was encouraged to flow. Thus, students would have greater freedom of choice in terms of content, products, etc., as long as high standards were met. Teachers would act as guides and facilitators.

- Students' creativity and curiosity would flow in expeditions or interdisciplinary projects on real life issues. These projects would last for several weeks at a minimum and result in very significant student work products.

Thus, ELOB promised that teachers would do much of the development of the curriculum units associated with the design. Over time as more teachers developed units with their classes, these units would be put on the Web and shared by all ELOB teachers. While each teacher might not develop all of his or her own units, he or she would have to develop at least one major expedition. Within these units students would be given choices and freedom to pursue their own interests. The CON design appeared to be most closely related to the ELOB design and philosophy.

MRSH stated it would provide for significant portions of curriculum based on E. D. Hirsch Core Knowledge or Advanced Placement courses, but teachers would still be responsible for developing interdisciplinary units (Hudson units) that would take up about one-third to one-half of the time of the student.

AC stated it would provide a scope and sequence for teachers in the form of learning purposes for each semester, but teachers would develop their own units within that framework. Students were given a great deal of freedom to set their own course on transdisciplinary projects known as "constructive actions." Like ELOB, the teacher would be the guide for the project but not dictate it to the students.

ATLAS fell somewhere in between. It advocated "a clearly articulated curriculum" that appeared to be based in traditional discipline standards. ATLAS schools would draw on the principle of "less is more." Curriculum would focus on essential questions that have the power to incite students' and teachers' imaginations and that flow from universal questions such as, "Where did I come from?" or "Why does the world look and behave as it does?" (ATLAS Proposal, 1992, p. 10). This implied some curriculum development by teachers, but its extent was very unclear.

One other major set of differences was evident even at this point in time. Some designs (RW and MRSH) described discipline-based curriculum—reading, math, social studies, and science—that matched their notions of standards. They tended to advocate relatively more traditional styles of instruction—or at least argued for "appropriate pedagogy" that did not throw away traditional pedagogy if it seemed the appropriate means for teaching that particular lesson. Others sought a much more interdisciplinary curriculum with traditional subjects no longer apparent (AC, CON, ELOB). Instruction was to be universally more progressive, and words such as *project-based, hands-on, and theme-driven* were used to describe the vast majority of the pedagogy. ATLAS and NARE appeared to fall somewhere in between with their positions less clearly delineated in the original proposals.

Only RW had specifically addressed basic skill development needs in its proposal. RW had already developed the Success for All reading program for teaching basic reading skills and wanted to develop a similar model for math skills. Other teams appeared to take for granted that children would learn the basic skills of reading and numerical literacy without a specifically developed reading or math program developed by the teams. They concentrated on more progressive curriculum and instruction notions to develop critical thinking or higher-order thinking skills in children.

Intervening Experiences

Three important factors influenced the development of the curriculum and instruction in the designs during the ensuing years. First, in the NAS partner districts, the teams worked with schools that tended to have a high percentage of students from impoverished backgrounds with low levels of academic achievement. The districts, therefore, were greatly concerned about basic skills acquisition in the elementary grades. Second, teacher time for curricular development was highly constrained and it remains unclear whether the teachers were well prepared from past experiences to develop new curriculum should they have the time to do so. Third, the teams concentrated their original efforts at development of elementary levels. In some cases, such as in Dade County and the San Antonio public schools, there were also high concentrations of students with English as a second language in the home. With the exception of some of the districts in Washington and Kentucky states, the major issue facing these partner districts was poor English acquisition. A major goal in undertaking an NAS partnership was to raise test scores on state assessments.

Within a year of working in these districts, district and school representatives became concerned over the lack of strong basic literacy and numeracy programs within most of the designs. In contrast, districts and schools became more interested in the Success for All program associated with the RW design.

Several districts took their own actions to remedy the situation. For example, San Antonio was primarily interested in raising its TAAS (Texas Assessment of Academic Skills) scores because of strong incentives in Texas to do so. The district mandated all schools adopt Everyday Math and schools also were told to adopt a basic literacy program from a menu supplied by the district. Schools were given no choice in this unless they could show they already had similarly effective programs in place. Among the NAS design-based schools only the RW schools were exempted from the literacy program rule.

But even they did not get exemptions from the Everyday Math program.   The result was low levels of implementation of the curricular and instruction components of the designs because of the mandated programs.   Cincinnati, Dade, and Memphis did not take quite such drastic actions but demanded or urged that design teams provide a complete literacy program as part of the design or adopt a proven one wholesale.

Design teams responded over a two-year period by creating their own programs, adopting existing programs, or creating lists of existing literacy and numeracy programs that were acceptable or complementary to the design.   With adoption of literacy and numeracy programs designs moved toward more specified curriculum and instructional strategies in the lower grades with less need for teacher development and more traditional subject breakdowns.

Those designs that advocated a strong role for teachers in the development of the curriculum and instructional units faced further challenges.   Many of the schools these designs worked with faced extremely restricted teacher time for development (Bodilly, 1998). Teachers were already overwhelmed with training in the design and working on committees required by the designs.   Their ability to create thoughtful and workable units was constrained by these limits.   This time issue arose more often when schools did not quite understand the commitment they were making to curriculum development when they accepted the designs, and several schools experienced backlashes against the design after they understood too late the level of effort required (Bodilly, 1998).

In addition, even as early as the demonstration phase, three designs (ATLAS, CON, ELOB) faced an additional challenge of ensuring a scope and sequence among the interdisciplinary units in the schools. This issue was not as evident in designs that came in with scope and sequences from standards (MRSH, RW) or from the design (AC).   But for the others, the demonstration phase had resulted in a plethora of uncoordinated curricular units within the school.   As one parent put it, "How many years in a row will my child visit the zoo and study the environment?   What about geology, history, etcetera?"

Furthermore, the designs that relied on teacher-developed curriculum units (AC, ATLAS, ELOB, CON, MRSH) needed to set up strong quality controls on these units. Schools and districts began to ask even in the demonstration phase, "Did the units measure up?"

The design teams responded to these calls for improvement over several years by ensuring a scope and sequence and by developing quality controls for the locally developed units. Different approaches were taken—most have teacher teams develop a scope and sequence for the curriculum in the first year, if one is not evident in the district standards. ELOB has teachers within the school review curricular units as part of a peer review process, while MRSH instituted a screening function by the team as well as one by the school.

By 1998, the designs requiring teacher-developed curriculum showed significant headway. For example, by Summer 1998 ELOB had published an annotated bibliography that contained more than 200 K–9 units or expeditions that were assessed as high quality (Grooms, 1998). Many of these units were available on the Web, and teachers could access them as exemplars in the process of building their own units or take them and adapt them to their own uses. MRSH and CON have similar bibliographic systems in place with access to units through the Internet or through the design team. In addition, the training provided to teachers by all the teams on unit development now contains clear standards for the units, "how-to manuals" for the building of units, and quality control mechanisms.[5]

Thus, the teams moved from rhetorical ideas in the proposal, through a rough development, to a well-supported system of interdisciplinary units and development support. In this sense then, the designs have matured to the point that extensive development by each school or each teacher is no longer needed. Nevertheless, some unit development is still required as part of the professional development of teachers by AC, ATLAS, CON, ELOB, and MRSH.

Finally, the development of units and instructional approaches seemed to focus most heavily on the elementary grades. In many cases this occurred because the design teams chose to develop their

---

[5]For example, ELOB has a 155-page manual, *Guide for Planning a Learning Expedition* (ELOB, 1998), that serves to inform teachers of the process.

curriculum and instructional strategies sequentially from lower grades to higher grades, even if they were working in higher grades at the time.[6] The designs also often started as pilots within the large high schools common to these districts; therefore, a complete curriculum was not initially needed. As indicated before, the districts were primarily interested in improving test scores on basic skills, so their focus and pressure were on the lower grades as well. The bottom line is that districts, schools, and teams agreed that the design teams have more completely developed curriculum and instructional strategies for the elementary levels than for the higher grade levels at this time.

Curriculum and Instruction as of 1998

The very significant original contrasts in curriculum and instructional approaches among the teams still remain; see Table 3.3.

In an example of planned development, several designs developed relatively prescriptive curriculum structures for teachers to use (AC's scope and sequence, MRSH Core Knowledge and Advanced Placement components, RW's heavily specified curriculum in all subjects). For the RW design this included a significant portion of curriculum dedicated to basic skills instruction and was a complete package.

For all others some part of the curriculum is still developed by teachers. The AC, ATLAS, CON, ELOB, and MRSH designs have, through planned development and adaptation to teacher needs, developed packages of units that reduce the need for new schools and teachers to develop curriculum units. Nevertheless, some unit development is still required as part of the professional development of teachers, but the development of an entire curriculum in each school is no longer an issue.

---

[6]For example, MRSH chose to develop its Hudson units and its "Water Shed" assessment for the elementary grades first, then the middle and high school grades.

STUDENT GROUPING AND INDIVIDUALIZED SERVICES

Student grouping and the move toward individualized services similar to that currently provided to Special Education children overlap with the curriculum and instructional element. Here the focus is on numbers of students facing a teacher or vice versa, the sequence of progressing from one teacher to another, and placement into classrooms.

Student Grouping and Individualized Services in the Original Proposals

The original proposals focused heavily on issues of grouping students within a school and within classrooms with heavy emphasis on detracking, mainstreaming, and small-group instruction; see Table 3.4. Several designs also advocated more unusual notions such as looping, multi-age classrooms, and schools divided into smaller houses. Different mechanisms were advocated.

- **All teams advocated the removal of tracking in schools.** In the proposals, tracking referred to the systematic and permanent assignment of children to ability-based groups. Tracking practices put all children "perceived" to have a similar ability level into the same classrooms over the school day. The detracking proposed by design teams required children to interact more often with children with different ability levels. In addition, some designs specifically required mainstreaming of Special Education students. As the RW design proposal put it, "Where are the special education classes at Wright School? Where are the Chapter 1 classes? There aren't any. All students who would ordinarily be in special or remedial classes are integrated in regular classes" (p. 10).

- **Teams differed in their support for homogeneous grouping by ability for learning certain tasks.** RW advocated that the children be placed in homogeneous ability groups for reading and math, but these groups would not be the same—one would be based on reading ability and the other on math ability. The children would be in heterogeneous groups throughout the rest

Table 3.3

Curriculum and Instruction Changes

Team	Proposal 1992	Design Materials 1998	Reason for Change
AC	• Purpose centered, organized in semester-long themes driven by student choice • Includes constructive actions • Teachers develop units based on detailed guidance on scope, sequence, and content of units • Transdisciplinary	*Same, except:* • Accept district-mandated literacy or math components • Offer more fully developed model units and notions of constructive actions	• Planned development • Adapt to district mandates • Adapt to student needs
ATLAS	• Clearly articulated, K–12 curriculum with locally developed scope and sequence • Based on traditional disciplines • Use of essential questions • Teacher developed	*Same, except:* • Accept district-mandated literacy or math components, or others identified as compatible • Offer more fully developed essential questions	• Planned development • Adapt to district mandate • Adapt to student needs
CON	• Interdisciplinary with combination of seminars and thematic projects • Heavy use of technology to access resources, develop products, etc. • Teacher developed	*Same, except:* • Accept district-mandated literacy and math components or others identified as compatible • Seminars dropped, then resurrected • Offer more fully developed curriculum units for sharing across sites	• Planned development • Adapt to district mandate • Adapt to student needs
ELOB	• Almost completely interdisciplinary, project-based curriculum • Composed of long-term "expeditions" • Driven by student choice • Teacher developed	*Same, except:* • Accept district-mandated literacy or math components or others identified as compatible • Offer more fully developed, exemplary curriculum units, bibliography of teacher-developed units and concept of fieldwork	• Planned development • Adapt to district mandates • Adapt to student needs
MRSH	• Foundation units that integrated disciplines, skills, and core knowledge developed by teachers • Secondary: Advanced Placement curriculum	*Same, except:* • Accept nonintegrated district-mandated literacy or math components • Offer more fully developed curriculum units to share across sites	• Planned development • Adapt to district mandate
NARE	• Appropriate local, teacher-developed curriculum tied to New Standards and assessment including work skills and technology	• Team in process of developing a K–12 curriculum package aligned with team-developed standards and assessment	• Reconceptualization • Adapt to teacher needs
RW	• Reading, math, and interdisciplinary components tied to MSPAP, completely developed by design team	*Same, except:* • No longer tied to MSPAP	• Planned development • Adapt to district mandates

Table 3.4

Grouping and Personalization Changes

Team	Proposal 1992	Design Materials 1998	Reason for Change
AC	• Detracking • Appropriate grouping with increased small-group instruction • Block schedule	• No change	
ATLAS	• Detracking • Appropriate grouping with increased small-group instruction • Reduced class size • Houses • Block scheduling	*Same, except:* • Dropped houses • De-emphasize small class size and detracking	• Planned development • Adapt to district norms • Reconceptualization
CON	• Detracking • Appropriate grouping with increased small-groups • Looping, multi-age • IEP • Reduced class size • Block schedule • School subdivided into houses	*Same, except:* • De-emphasize detracking • Dropped looping, multi-age, and houses to encourage "appropriate grouping" • Dropped IEC and reduced class size	• Planned development • Adapt to district norms • Reconceptualization
ELOB	• Detracking • Heterogeneous grouping with increase in small groups • Looping • IEP • Reduced school size • Flexible schedule	*Same, except:* • Dropped multi-age, IEC	• Planned development • Adapt to district norms • Reconceptualization
MRSH	• Detracking • Performance grouping • Looping • Strong tutoring component • IEC computer-based • Increase in small groups • Appropriate flexible schedule	*Same, except:* • De-emphasized detracking • Dropped looping, and small groups in favor of schools deciding appropriate grouping • De-emphasize computer-based IEC • Tutoring optional	• Planned development • Adapt to district norms
NARE	• Detracking • To be determined by school based on research	• Block schedule; elementary 2.5 hours of ready and unity. 1 hour math • Looping for 3 years • Assistance for at-risk students • Flexible schedule • 9–12 house system • Tutoring • Summer school	• Reconceptualization
RW	• Homogeneous grouping in reading and math based on diagnostics every 8–9 weeks • Heterogeneous grouping in other disciplines • Mix of large groups, small groups, cooperative learning • Strong tutoring during and after school • Specified block schedule • IEP • Multi-age	*Same, except:* • Reduced emphasis in after-school tutoring • Dropped multi-age	• Planned development

of the day. The grouping would not be permanent but based on frequently assessed improvement. ATLAS, CON, and MRSH used phrases such as "appropriate grouping for the learning task" to express their philosophy. In contrast, ELOB was staunchly against such practices, advocating heterogeneous groupings across the board.

• **Some teams advocated looping or multi-year assignment to a specific teacher.** CON, ELOB, and MRSH supported two- to three-year groupings of student and teachers to avoid dehumanization of the student, to promote knowledge of the student's individual needs, and to reduce the wasted time of "getting to know you" at the beginning of each school year. In the MRSH design this concept is specifically linked to the curriculum, instructional practices, and standards for graduation. Students would remain in a group until the child mastered the knowledge necessary for promotion. The design saw time spent in a grade as no longer a given, but dependent upon a child's progress in self-paced learning.

• **Some teams advocated multi-age groupings of students.** CON, ELOB, MRSH, and RW all advocated the grouping of children into clusters of ages. ELOB and RW were specific about the ages for the clusters; MRSH simply referred to these as primary, elementary, and upper-division groupings.

• **Two teams advocated tutoring.** RW and MRSH required formal tutoring programs within the school for students who were not keeping up or who needed extra help. RW insisted on tutors in each classroom as well as after-school tutoring. "Instead, Chapter 1 and special education resource services will be provided after school by the school's regular staff. During the after school time some students will receive tutoring from teachers or aides, some will receive peer tutoring and others will provide peer tutoring to younger children. In addition, a latch-key program will be offered to provide children of working parents with supervised play, art, music, and time and help with homework" (RW Proposal, pp. 23–24).

• **Three teams talked of Individual Education Compacts or Plans as the means to follow specific students and create individualized instructional programs.** CON, ELOB, and MRSH each advocated the development of an individualized student education plan for each and every student. These plans were to be jointly developed by teachers, parents, and students.[7] Each advocated computer-based systems that could be easily accessed and updated. For MRSH and CON the students themselves would be privy to the data so as to get immediate feedback on their status.

- **Teams advocated reduced class size or school size.** ATLAS and CON required reduced class sizes. Both teams also advocated dividing up a large school into smaller clusters of permanent faculty that could better provide individualized services to students. ELOB advocated a school size of no more than 350 students (ELOB Proposal, p. 14).

- **All advocated the use of smaller groups within the classroom.** All of the teams advocated the use of small-group instruction as the means toward more individualized curriculum and instruction, but also appropriate socialization and cooperative learning. Some were very specific about the size; for example, ELOB insisted on no more than 25 students per "guide" (ELOB Proposal, p. 14).

Intervening Experiences

As with the elements already discussed, the experience during demonstration and scale-up changed the designs because of the conflicts with existing policies or procedures or difficulty in convincing teachers that these concepts would have positive effects.

Perhaps the most significant change was backing away from multi-age and multi-year groupings. Experiences in demonstration schools indicated that many teachers, not all, rejected these concepts and in many cases simply refused to implement them. In other cases, the teachers challenged the design teams to substantiate a research base that supported these concepts in the universal terms dictated by the teams; several teams did review their research base. Review of the literature and the practical difficulty of implementation led several

---

[7]Another indication of some amount of student choice in learning.

teams to drop this notion. For example, RW dropped the idea of multi-year groupings within the development year. CON and MRSH changed their language to include these concepts as part of a review of possible strategies to use, but left it up to the school to decide on "appropriate groupings." For example, CON's original proposal said:

> A typical cluster will consist of half a dozen teachers and a hundred or more students with an age range of up to four years (e.g., a cluster might have students in the range 6 to 10 years of age). Teachers in the cluster will have special responsibility for a group of approximately twenty students, for whom they will act as a special adviser and friend over a period of several years. (p. 12)

Its current materials state, "To ensure stable classroom cultures and a continuity of norms and relationships from one year to the next, students may stay with the same teachers for two or more years" (CON Profile, p. 1). There is no mention of multi-age groupings. Only ELOB has held firmly and steadfastly to the concept of looping.

Other concepts for grouping still remain in the designs, but are less emphasized. For example, tracking is still attacked, but only two designs have kept up the vigor of the language as well as the intensity of the push in implementation to remove it from the schools—ELOB and RW. Others have taken a more philosophical approach in the face of parental support for separate classes for talented and gifted students or teacher responses to abolishing ability-based groupings. While they are against it and remain dedicated to removing it from their schools, they recognize it is a long-term prospect. Implementation of other components will come long before implementation of a detracked system.

Efforts toward individual education compacts or programs have made headway, but as mentioned in the assessment section, have been held up by the excessive amount of time it takes to actually maintain the data system needed. Thus, IECs/IEPs are still part of three designs but are less emphasized in practical implementation.

Similarly the tutoring component has become vaguer or less ambitious due to the realities of schools. For example, the original RW proposal envisioned before- and after-school tutoring with transportation offered to students (p. 8). Students would also have one-on-one tutoring in the classroom through the use of resource teachers available through Title I funds and managed by the family support coordinator with recommendations by teachers for tutoring of specific students in specific areas. But the reality faced by schools often prevents this component from being implemented due to resource and transportation constraints. While the classroom tutoring remains a vital part of the design, the before- and after-school tutoring has basically disappeared from the design (Slavin et al., 1996, pp. 73–88). In districts with preexisting tutoring programs, the design works to improve that system.

Perhaps the most successful regrouping in implementation and in the strength of statements in the current design documents is the use of smaller groupings within the classroom. The reason for this success and continuity is straightforward: This component was supported by all the teams and hence built into their curriculum and instructional strategies. The hands-on, project-based instruction of many designs or the cooperative learning embedded in the RW design served to promote small-group instruction and vice versa.

Student Grouping as of 1998

The groupings originally advocated by designs have changed somewhat with several being dropped and many now referred to as principles to work toward as opposed to ideas to aggressively implement. This change occurred in large part because designs learned that these groupings were not essential to the designs and because teachers simply were not convinced of their value and did not implement them. Those groupings and assignments deemed essential to and confluent with other important elements of the design survived. Those that were not or that prevented implementation of the whole design were put on a back burner for later consideration or are now referred to as "principles" to be worked toward rather than essential elements to be immediately implemented. The language in many proposals changed from strident confidence about a particular grouping arrangement to advocating "flexible" or "appropriate" grouping as determined by the school. Smaller class sizes and smaller schools were not a possibility in most districts in which the teams worked.

However, several grouping ideas remain strong, including the commitment to multi-year looping in ELOB, detracking and mainstreaming in ELOB and RW, and small-group instruction across all designs. The "appropriate" or "flexible" stance allows for further distinctions within a design by locality—schools of the same design might vary significantly in their grouping arrangement both across and within districts, with the few exceptions noted above.

As with other components, these design changes led to the possibility of a great deal of site variation among schools using designs, while leaving it likely that all NAS-design related schools would have more small-group pedagogy. These changes have also led to the probability that conflicts will exist between the grouping component and other components of the design.

GOVERNANCE

Not all designs addressed governance. Those that did were forceful and in some cases very prescriptive about the nature of governance. Those who were silent on this issue have remained largely silent. Those who were forceful have revised their stances in a similar manner to that discussed above—from strong prescriptive statements to principles to work toward.

Governance in the Original Proposals

The issue of governance clearly lit the fire of some proposals, but virtually all of them criticized the existing bureaucracy and its negative effect on schools and teachers. Most called for significant school-level control of specific functions—often referred to in the proposals as "school autonomy." The organizational literature might call it "decentralization." Three teams in particular (ATLAS, CON, and MRSH) saw significant governance changes as central to their designs. Others were less adamant, calling for modest changes (AC, ELOB, RW). Overall,

- **Several designs required the development of school-level governing teams.** In all cases these teams were to be participatory in nature—including teachers and parents. ATLAS was very specific about the need for inclusion while other teams were less so.

- **Student advisory teams or committees.** RW called for the establishment of a committee of relevant persons who could quickly identify student problems and assign the proper caseworker from among the schools' staff; this committee was part of the "relentless" approach advocated by RW.

- **Governing committees.** ATLAS advocated a series of committees as well, but they were not just for developing plans. Rather they would govern the school.[8] CON called for clusters of teachers to govern the school, with each group of teachers having autonomy over their budget and the planning for their grades. (Recall CON required a school divided into clusters of multi-age, multi-year student groupings led by a few teachers.) The pilot schools RW worked with in Maryland already had School Improvement Teams that guided the implementation of the design and made policy decisions (RW Proposal, p. 26).

- **Teacher teams.** All designs called for the establishment of regular teacher teams to address student needs, plan curriculum and instruction within a grade or series of grades, and to generally work collaboratively together. This plan was most evident in the AC, ATLAS, CON, and ELOB designs. In the CON design these teacher teams actually made up the governance structure of the school.

- **All teams emphasized significant autonomy, but some were more ambitious than others.**

  - **Three teams sought "appropriate" autonomy to implement the design.** AC, ELOB, and RW did not say very much about the autonomy needed, but much was implied in their proposals. AC, ELOB, and RW were designed to work within the existing system if the school was given certain authorities, especially over its curriculum and allocation of funds within the school. For RW in particular a school required control over its Title I funds in order to adopt the design. While ELOB did not demand new governance, it sought relief from the current testing regime and sought a stronger role for teachers and parents in governing the

---

[8]ATLAS uses the term *pathway* to indicate a geographic feeder pattern of middle schools and elementary schools feeding into a high school.

school. The teacher role was not specified, but the emphasis on the growing authority and responsibilities of teachers within that school was clear. In addition, the design promoted the use of participatory structures to enable adult learning and development of new roles. In the terms of the proposal the design wanted a "web structure instead of a rigid hierarchy" and "responsibility pushed down the organizational ladder" (ELOB Proposal, p. 27). AC said, "the team does not specify how schools should reorganize their policies and practices to institute these changes" (AC proposal, p. 19).

— **Three sought complete control over budget, staffing, curriculum, and instruction.** For ATLAS this autonomy was at the pathway level, with all schools within each pathway to become an autonomous governing unit or minidistrict within the larger district. As the proposal put it: "We would like to think that ATLAS schools could exist within the current policy environment, but our experience has shown that to be possible only in rare circumstances" (ATLAS Proposal, p. 26). For MRSH autonomy would be centered at the school with the principal as CEO, although even in its proposal, MRSH saw significant regulatory barriers to its design. "Our design includes features that may require changes in existing federal, state, and local regulations; a major activity during Phase 1 will be to identify the specific regulatory obstacles and to request the necessary waivers from appropriate agencies" (MRSH Proposal, p. iii). For CON autonomy would be centered on clusters of teachers below the school level.

— **Two sought parental choice for schools.** MRSH specifically stated that parents be given a choice as to whether to attend the MRSH schools. CON indicated that parents should be able to choose which cluster within the school their children would attend.

Intervening Experiences

Early in the demonstration phase it became clear that schools did not have the autonomy required by some designs. Neither would districts always allow schools to have the required autonomy (Bodilly et al., 1996). During the demonstration phase, which focused on just one or two schools in a district, some districts agreed to let a school have significant autonomy—it was, after all, seen as an experiment with only one or two schools. Certainly schools in the demonstration phase were given autonomy over curriculum and instruction. But seldom, even under these pilot conditions, were schools given authority over budget and staffing.

By the end of the demonstration phase, CON had completely revised its governance structure. A school design team replaced the autonomous clusters within the school. The school design team would plan and enact the implementation of the design and would report to the principal or governing committee. Eventually, this design team might fuse and become one with the participatory governance committee. Meanwhile, clusters remained but did not have the autonomy or governance power once advocated.

In the same time period, MRSH established planning committees of teachers and others to develop school plans for implementation. For MRSH this was a series of committees in six different school areas. For example, a technology committee would develop a technology plan, and a professional development committee would develop a professional development plan for the school to follow over the next several years. A governance committee would work toward the more participatory governance for the school and school-level autonomy that the design required.

This lack of school-level control and concessions by districts even in the demonstration phase led NAS to propose its district strategy for the scale-up phase. That strategy was centered on a district commitment to: (1) restructure in support of school-level control over curriculum, instruction, budget, staffing, standards, and professional development; (2) adopt a decentralized governance structure; and (3) require transformation within five years of over 30 percent of the schools using designs. Perhaps most important, NAS proposed that districts allow all the teams to work in the district.

Table 3.5

Governance and Staffing

Team	Proposal 1992	Design Materials 1998	Reason for Change
AC	• School autonomy appropriate to implement design—largely curriculum • Required full-time facilitator • Required one hour per day teacher-team meetings	• Work with district to implement design • Facilitator can be part-time • Meetings encouraged, but not required	• Adapt to district governance
ATLAS	• Pathway concept of autonomous feeder pattern • School autonomy over budget, staffing, standards, curriculum, and instruction • Cross-school committees articulate standards, scope, and sequence • Within-school committee governs school • Teacher teams	• Reduced emphasis on full autonomy, district/school co-management • Slightly changed committee structure • Heavier emphasis on teacher study teams	• Planned development • Adapt to district governance • Reconceptualization
CON	• School autonomy over budget, staffing, standards, curriculum, and instruction • Teachers organized in multi-grade clusters with autonomy over cluster • Possible requirement for technology coordinator • Parental choice of cluster	• Reduced emphasis on autonomy, work within district constraints • Teacher clusters not autonomous • No mention of parental choice	• Adapt to district governance
ELOB	• School autonomy appropriate to implement design • Teachers organized in multi-age teams collaborate as professionals to increase role in governing school	No change	
MRSH	• Complete school autonomy from district • Strong principal role with support from specified teacher planning teams • Parental choice of school	• Reduced emphasis on autonomy, work with district to support appropriate level of autonomy	• Adapt to district governance

NARE	• Develop a system of Total Quality Management (TQM) for schools
	• Work with state and district partners to:
	  • Enact finance reform
	  • Remove legal and regulatory barriers to TQM
	  • Enact incentives for high performance
	  • Create Master Teachers Certificate and develop Master Teacher
		Recommends and will provide:
		• School review and monitoring system
		• Resource allocation system
		• Support for low-performing schools
		• Accountability system
		
		Schools will have:
		• Site council
		• Leadership and Management Team
		• Substantial autonomy over budget
		• Design coach
		• Full time literary coordinator in K–5
		• Community Outreach Coordinator
			• Reconceptualization

RW	• School autonomy appropriate to implement design—control over Title I funds • School improvement council to advise principal • Student advisory teams • Required full-time facilitator and full-time family support coordinator	*Same, except:* • Part-time family support coordinators acceptable, in small schools use part-time facilitator	• Adapt to district governance

For example, Memphis City Schools committed to the district strategy using eight different designs—some from NAS as well as Paidaeia, Montessori, and Accelerated Schools. The district, and others in similar circumstances, was reluctant to hand over the reins of control to schools given: (1) the diverse range of circumstances in each school;   (2) the large number of schools involved; and (3) the diverse range of design team requirements given the number of design teams. Furthermore, Tennessee state law dictated some of the internal staffing relationships in schools, and Tennessee had also recently passed a class size reduction law that had to be carefully implemented and monitored by the district. From the district point of view the school could not be allowed staffing, hiring, and firing autonomy. Finally, the district was the lowest performing in the state on state assessments. While willing to experiment, the district also had to ensure that test scores rose. Perhaps understandably then, the district agreed to move slowly toward the NAS vision of a decentralized district.

Similar stories could be told for each of the districts NAS and its teams worked in. The story was perhaps even more complicated for those districts with strong union contracts that curtailed the district from even making staffing and hiring decisions without consultation and for those districts with significant budget crises that had to control their budgets for the time being.

Governance and Staffing as of 1998

We have already indicated that control over standards, assessments, curriculum, and instruction have been maintained in large part by districts—in some districts design teams and their schools have a great deal of leeway; in other districts they have little. This argument also holds for autonomy over budget and staffing of the schools. Control over the budget is absolutely essential to design implementation—even for designs that did not originally address this issue. For example, implementation of any design requires substantial investment in materials and professional development as well as permanent restructuring of these funds (Keltner, 1998). Some designs require new staffing or positions within the schools; without expenditures for these positions and removal of others the design cannot be implemented. Over time several districts associated with

NAS promoted site-level budgeting, making this a reality in some NAS schools. However, staffing autonomy has not been freely granted to design teams and their schools (Bodilly, 1998) and is especially difficult in districts with strong unions.

Given this experience, the scale-up phase could be seen as a test to determine just how much school-level autonomy was actually needed to implement the basics of a given design. Teams have moderated their design documents to be less strident about governance changes up front. The end goals remain the same for the teams, but documents reveal a more gradual process for achieving autonomy and the ability to function as a design-based school even in conditions of curtailed autonomy. Overall,

- Design descriptions do not now ask for blanket, up-front school-level autonomy. Experience with districts has led to each adopting a more prolonged period of negotiation with the district over this issue and much more detailed descriptions of what autonomy is needed and why.

- All designs have become more explicit in their materials and in negotiations with districts and schools concerning the autonomy and governance changes needed. As an example, RW has very specific materials concerning the need for school-level control over Title I funds and the need for continuous acquisition of materials. ELOB has become more specific about the need for control over professional development funds.

- All designs accept existing standards and assessments.

- All designs now work around district-mandated programs.

- Several teams outline processes for gaining further autonomy as design implementation progresses (ATLAS, CON, MRSH). Their materials are much more explicit about what control is needed and when it is needed than they were in the past. The committee structures of ATLAS and MRSH have changed somewhat and their time lines for achieving this goal have lengthened.

In the end, we again see adaptation to conflicts with local policy causing a shift toward considerable local variation even within a design. An MRSH school in Memphis might by now have control over its own budget; one in San Antonio certainly does not. But the principles of school-level autonomy, and in ATLAS the pathway autonomy, remain within the design documents, even as they vary significantly in real implementation. In addition, we see that concessions made on this element prevented the implementation of other elements and led to significant revision of the designs. These revisions have resulted in the strong possibility of incoherence and inconsistency within and between design-based schools.

COMMUNITY INVOLVEMENT AND SUPPORT

At the time of the original proposals Kentucky had just passed legislation integrating social services at the school level through family resource centers. James Comer had proposed and was implementing in New Haven (Conn.) his ideas on community health teams centered in the school and integrating social services on-site. Thus, it should be no surprise that some of the teams were very vocal on this issue—calling for strong support for integrated health and social services at the school building level.

Community Involvement and Support in the Original Proposals

Originally five designs envisioned the school as a focus for community involvement in public life and the provision of social services to families; see Table 3.6. Five designs, ATLAS, ELOB, MRSH, NARE, and RW, advocated significant integration at the school-building level of support services for students and their families. One design, CON, was almost silent on this matter. And one design, AC, took a curricular view of community involvement— students would be responsible for developing community projects as part of their understanding of and contribution to the world in which they lived.

In the group of five designs with strong support for significant integration at the school-building level, ATLAS took perhaps the most extreme view. The design proposal stated that, "especially in poorer communities many parents and teachers are uncomfortable communicating with each other and schools are disconnected from the health care, housing, legal assistance, and child care services that are supposed to support the diverse developmental pathways of low income students" (ATLAS Proposal, p. 18). Its vision stated that "ATLAS communities can bridge the gaps between home, school, and needed services and work" (p. 18). In particular it called for:

- Building a community health team that would "fashion school-based services so that students no longer have to choose between coming to school and meeting their other critical needs" (p. 19).

- "The Parent Participation Team may expand to match students to community members who can act as mentors to students" (p. 19).

- Surveying community resources and creating a plan for a more integrated community of learners.

For ATLAS, the governance structure was key to making the connections to community that were needed to support student learning. Over several years the expectations were that the school would be the site for the provision of integrated social services for all families in the community, and that the committee structure of the design would encourage inclusion of all stakeholders, thereby strengthening the community itself.

While ELOB did not have so highly developed a committee structure, it too advocated the school as the site for social services provision. "We hope to offer parents an array of social services on site. . . . We would rather help make time for a single parent by bringing the family care provider or social worker to the school site, instead of keeping agencies and family help at bay and creating transportation and logistical hardships for parents" (ELOB Proposal, p. 29).

On a rhetorical level the RW proposal advocated significant collaboration of social service providers with the schools. It wrote of "careful planning by social service agencies, community developers, and the school and community leadership to empower local citizens to act together to support the well-being of the county's families and their children" (RW Proposal, p. 9). More practically, RW required a family support coordinator as part of the school design, whose job was to ensure that all students arrived on time and ready to learn. The coordinator's job would not be to ensure integrated social services for the family but to ensure the provision of support for the students.   RW adapted the Comer model of a school-level community health team.

MRSH was interested in community support but largely confined it to ensuring that students entered schools ready to learn. "Hudson schools will work with parents and community agencies to assure that all children have an equal chance of attaining the high achievement standards we will be setting for our students. We will accomplish this in three ways: (1) by defining readiness standards for enrollment; (2) by forming a consortium of existing pre-school providers that will adequately prepare students to meet these standards; and (3) by helping parents with responsibilities to ready their children for school" (MRSH Proposal, p. 26).

In general, these four teams (ATLAS, ELOB, MRSH, and RW) can be seen as advocating some integration at the school-building level of support services for students, with the extent of the school role varying among them.

In contrast, the CON proposal used the term *community* largely to refer to the communities or clusters of teachers that it advocated within the school, not the larger community surrounding the school.

Finally, AC proposed a much more organic curricular approach to community in its section "The Community Becomes a Part of the Educational Process" (AC Proposal, p. 21). In conversations, Audrey Cohen referred to students in her schools as "ambassadors to the world." The entire curriculum model was based on purposeful learning, and that purpose was always for students to find the means to put their newly found knowledge to use in service to the community. Thus, rather than the school being the focus of social service provision by government agencies, the students became the providers of community services. "These young people along with their fellow students, teachers, parents and even principals are making their school a vital resource to the community" (p. 1). The community becomes a resource for the student's learning, but what could students provide? Actual examples include:

- Second graders with a learning purpose of "We use government to improve our community" would measure traffic load and speed in front of their school, eventually writing a report and presenting it to the local governing unit requesting a speed bump in front of the school to slow traffic.

- Students would explore different painting techniques used through the ages. In teams, they would paint several canvases and deliver these to the police commissioner on opening day of the new police building. The canvases would decorate the halls along with researched descriptions of the different techniques used.

Whether the students participated in cleaning up a local beach or mailed care packages to children in other parts of the world hit by disasters, the point was to build a better community by student learning and informed action.

The proposal indicated that increasing student community-based actions would allow better community services to follow. "In a school that allies itself so closely to the community, it makes sense to draw those community services that support education into the school. In addition to this primary goal, the inclusion of such services will help younger children to understand what a community is and what basic needs the community serves" (p. 23). In short, community services and integration, if attempted at all, would fill an educational need of the students.

Intervening Experiences

The experiences in the following years proved to be important in shaping this element. Several different influences emerged.

First and perhaps most important, the design teams that focused on integrated social services provision at the school level (especially ATLAS and ELOB) soon realized the difficulties involved in managing change across public agencies with diverse views of a problem and trapped by specific program directives. School-level people and parents do not have the time or the expertise by and large to take on the "bureaucracy" of the entire social services network (Smrekar, 1994), especially teachers and principals in the midst of curricular and instructional changes. These teams soon recognized that the school's ability to carry out this vision was limited; it required strong commitment by the entire political community to do so.

In current design documents, ATLAS still holds to its vision and has developed new team structures to enable it. The survey of resources in the community is one of the first steps toward this as part of the first-year implementation plan. However, ATLAS began to take a more opportunistic approach to enable, encourage, and help schools take advantage of opportunities that presented themselves over time, but not to confront this issue head-on. Like other concessions, this would lead to significant local variation in implementation.

The integrated social services element is largely invisible now in ELOB documents but has taken on a new function, which we will discuss below.

RW and MRSH, with less ambitious visions, managed more consistent progress. In 1994 and 1995, MRSH published materials designed for parents to help in early child care and to ensure children were ready to learn (MRSH 1994, 1995a). Through its committee structure it found ways to begin the process of identifying and improving local child care providers and identifying mentoring resources. Its implementation materials support this function as does some of its training provision (MRSH, 1995b). Likewise RW, when granted autonomy over the Title I funds, could ensure the creation of its family support coordinator position in the school. While initially this coordinator position was not well defined, over several years, the team developed materials to guide the job and training programs for the position (Slavin et al., 1996, chapter 6).

Second, it became clear early on in scale-up that design teams could not enable schools to create integrated social services without other conditions at the site being present, and that the predominant concern of the schools was parent involvement. The schools served were concerned about getting parents to ensure their children attended school and completed homework (Berends, 1999). From the schools' point of view that would be progress.

In response to this concern, design teams began to focus more on the development of programs to encourage parental participation in the schools. Many different forms now take place, depending on the design and the actual sites: parent involvement in governance as volunteers, as tutors, as resources to students on projects, and as members of community review panels for student work.

A third intervening factor was the completion of more of the interdisciplinary curriculum that the design teams had envisioned. In actual implementation observed during RAND site visits, the projects that students began to work on and products they produced often were community oriented. As those designs with student-driven curriculum developed further, students and teachers alike often found themselves in the community collecting data, interviewing people, identifying community problems to be solved, and sometimes helping to solve them. This student-based community involvement led inevitably to more of the community becoming involved in the schools—not through the PTA necessarily, but through the student projects. Interviews with teachers and parents during RAND site visits and review of curriculum projects and outcomes indicated that community visitors to the classrooms became more commonplace. Parent involvement in project work increased. Visits by the students to Web locations around the world in interactive exchanges increased. Actually experiencing the potential for what community involvement might mean led to a different conceptualization of the curricular component and the parental involvement component of several teams.

As an example, ELOB documents became much more specific about the nature of its expeditions. In 1995 it published a description of and clarification of what expeditions were meant to accomplish. Called "Fieldwork, An Expeditionary Learning Outward Bound Reader," Volume I, the document clarified what the team meant by earlier notions of taking the classroom outside of the school. The document distinguished between the field trips of the past and the "fieldwork" of ELOB students, which involved research and learning outside the school. It also emphasized the community involvement aspect of learning from the student point of view, describing actual student products in service of the community.

Likewise, the experiences of CON and AC began to emphasize both the potential positive impact of community work on the student as well as on the community itself. In CON much of this takes place through technology—broadcasting radio programs to the community, interacting with other sites on the Web, exploring community-based resources in this manner. Community service in AC and CON also takes place in person through project work. While this notion had been present in the AC design from the beginning, actual implementation allowed it to flower.

Community Involvement and Services as of 1998

The scale-up experiences caused teams to become much more pragmatic as opposed to visionary. A combination of adaptation to client needs (both students and teachers) and adaptation to conflicting policies and conditions caused design teams to rethink their ideas. Overall,

- All design documents and training now focus on very concrete, and more limited, actions schools can take regardless of the political climate of the city in which they function.

- Designs include parent involvement programs, community service projects, and sometimes facilitators at the school level who work with existing social service providers to help in specific student cases.

- The designs appear to have switched the focus from forcing changes in community support for health and human services for students to getting students practically involved in the betterment of the community, getting parents involved in their children's education, and working within the existing system to ensure that others provide for student needs.

In discussions concerning this element with most designs during this period, teams emphasized recognition of the important role that student-driven project-based learning could play in the development of community involvement, and recognition of the importance of community service as motivation for student learning. It should be no surprise then that by 1998, AC, ATLAS, CON, ELOB, and MRSH all required some community service project for graduation. Several required community service throughout the student's school experience.

Two teams, ELOB and RW, now say they had not intended to meet the vision set out in their proposal. They have indicated to us that they had oversold their intentions concerning these concepts because they believed it was required by the RFP.

Table 3.6

Community Involvement and Support

Team	Proposal 1992	Design Materials 1998	Reason for Change
AC	• Students as ambassadors to the community • Constructive action set in community • Speaker and volunteers in school • Community audit	*Same*	
ATLAS	• Integrated social services provided on campus • Community health team • Parent participation team • Community participation in governance structure • Survey of community needs and assets	*Same, except:* • Very reduced emphasis on integrated social services; opportunistic approach to local circumstances • Added community service project for graduation • Family centers	• Adapt to district and city policies
CON		• Added community service project for graduation	• Reconceptualization
ELOB	• Integrated social service provision on campus • Students learning in the community	• Dropped integrated social services • Added community projects in high school • Increased emphasis on students in the field	• Adapt to district and city policies
MRSH	• Ready-to-learn supports to parents	• Developed handbook on community involvement and support to aid schools	• Planned development
NARE	• Identify strategies to encourage public support • Completely integrated social services at school level supported by governance changes at the state and local levels (modeled on KY system). Includes pre-natal to 18. • Ready-to learn supports offered by schools	• Help school staff reach out to families to support student learning • Help school build safety net • Help school create community partners • School appoints community outreach coordinator	• Reconceptualization
RW	• Enable collaboration between social service providers and schools • Family support coordinator works with individual students and family to ensure student support • Community health team	*Same, except:* • Reduced emphasis on collaboration, rely on family support coordinator	• Adapt to district and city policies

The major exception to the above is LALC/ULC. While we do not include this team in most of this discussion, it is useful to note that it has very successfully developed this element in several of the demonstration sites and now has materials and concepts that can be used by other sites. Its integrated services model was most fully developed at its Elizabeth Street school, which is now visited by many schools and communities interested in replicating this concept.

PROFESSIONAL LIVES OF TEACHERS AND ROLE CHANGES

Professional development is critical for school improvement—how else, but through professional development, would the designs become implemented in the schools? Thus, the original designs all addressed the professional development of teachers, but this term had two distinct meanings depending upon the team.

Professional Lives of Teachers in Original Proposals

The original proposals contrasted in their approach to professional development; see Table 3.7. One set of designs (AC, MRSH, RW) discussed professional development in terms of training teachers to implement the designs. We call this a design training approach. Others (ATLAS, CON, ELOB, and NARE) talked more about the long-term development of each teacher's capability and professional life and how it would contribute to school improvement. It is no coincidence that these four designs required much more teacher development of curriculum and instructional strategies as part of the professionalization of teaching. In addition, they required extensive school-level autonomy over hiring, staff development, promotion, and firing.

Design training approaches. Some teams (AC, MRSH and RW) discussed professional development primarily in terms of the training needed by teachers to implement the design. The purpose of this training was to promote understanding of the design principles and to inculcate in teachers new habits of curriculum and instruction. Of the teams, they were the most specific in early phases

Table 3.7
Professional Development Changes

Team	Proposal 1992	Design Materials 1998	Reason for Change
AC	• Design training approach • Develop own curriculum consistent with AC design • Grade-level teams required 1 hour/day • Coordinator position full-time	• Retract from master teacher, meeting requirement and full-time coordinator • Add needs assessment activities	• Planned development • Adapt to district policies
ATLAS	• Professionalization approach • Teachers fully part of governance decisionmaking • Encouraged participation in governance and study teams • Opportunities for collaboration, networks, and further education • School autonomy over hiring staff development, and promotion • Teachers develop curriculum	• Add needs assessment activities • Generally, accepts less than full autonomy over school professional development • All teachers participate in study groups	• Planned development • Adapt to district policies • Adapt to teacher needs
CON	• Professionalization approach • Teachers in clusters, full autonomy of cluster • Teachers develop curriculum • Participation in networks	• Add needs assessment activities and benchmarking process • Participate in Critical Friends visits • Extensive networking opportunities • Sharing of curriculum units • Drop cluster autonomy, but keep cluster	• Planned development • Adapt to district policies • Adapt to teacher needs
ELOB	• Professionalization approach • Teachers required to develop curriculum • Extensive time for collaboration, further education • Built in 20 day/year for professional development • Encourage peer review	• Add needs assessment activities • Increase sharing of curriculum units • Publish the Web "newsletter" • Develop mechanisms for peer review	• Planned development • Adapt to teacher needs
MRSH	• Design training approach • Teachers develop part of curriculum • Master teachers, associate teachers, aides and apprentices • Autonomy over hiring, staff development, and promotion • More coherent & aligned with needs of school • Peer review of teacher and curriculum units	• Retract from hierarchy of teachers • Settle for less than full autonomy • Peer review of teaching dropped. Fuller development of curriculum review	• Planned development • Adapt to district policies • Adapt to teacher needs
NARE	• Professionalization approach • Teachers develop curriculum • Master teachers • New teacher certification • Accountability on assessments • Autonomy over hiring staff development and promotion	• Team provides curriculum • Retract from accountability, new incentives, and full autonomy • Encourage peer review	• Reconceptualization • Adapt to teacher needs
RW	• Design training approach • Grade-level teacher teams • Design team provides curriculum and instruction packages • Coordinator and family support positions	*Same*	

about what this would entail. Little attention was paid to professional development from other sources or long-term professional development of teachers.

This approach made sense for these three teams in that they tended to have more of the curriculum and instruction worked out for teachers than did other designs. For example, RW's intention was to provide teachers with the full curriculum and instructional content to cover grades K–5. Teachers did not have to learn how to develop curriculum nor did they have to use excessive judgment as to which instructional approaches to use. The design team would provide this. Thus, the professional development of the teachers was grounded in becoming fluent in the curriculum and instructional strategies provided.

AC did not provide the full curriculum but did provide a scope and sequence for each semester and extensive materials on units and how to develop them. As the proposal put it, "To enable them to make a running head start with the new system, we will prepare a comprehensive set of curriculum materials for the schools, including examples, of possible Constructive Actions relating to each Purpose, and sample lessons plans. . . . We plan to train master teachers to help others teach in the comprehensive way this design required and assume the new roles for which it calls" (p. 20). This team saw teachers slowly over time adopting the design as the idea of purposeful learning took hold in the school. The team proposed a week of fairly extensive whole staff training to get the process started. The extensive materials provided would sustain teachers in their development.

Not coincidentally, both these designs saw limited changes to the governance structure of the schools. They did not seek out new roles for teachers as a whole but focused the teachers on what went on in their classrooms. While both proposed grade-level team meetings on a regular basis to share ideas and discuss student progress, teacher teams were not meant to be the means for collegial development.

Finally, these two teams did see some changes for a limited number of teachers. For example, the RW and AC designs require a school-level design facilitator. Both designs increase dramatically the number of volunteers in the school—but do not change the role of the teacher. This person is responsible for helping design implementation. In addition, RW has a family support coordinator with specific functions, and the design describes new roles for the Title I resource teachers, and training is provided.

For MRSH, a major part of the curriculum was dictated by the team—Core Knowledge, workplace skills and cultural literacy. While teachers would be responsible for development of interdisciplinary units, much of the curriculum would be predetermined. Finally, MRSH did elaborate on new roles for teachers, but this was largely a hierarchical delineation among the teaching staff—master teachers, associate teachers, and aides and apprentices. The master teachers would take on new roles as mentors, peer reviewers, and so on. Professional development was specifically defined as a program of training for the staff in the design elements (pp. 12–14).

School-based professionalization approaches. Three other teams (ATLAS, CON, and ELOB) contrasted sharply with this approach. They talked more about professional development in terms of the long-term development of each teacher's capability and professional life and how it would contribute to school-level improvement. They did not address it specifically as training in the design but rather addressed the need for teacher development through "collaboration," "ongoing experiences," "peer review,"[9] and "involvement in networks outside the school."

They envisioned seriously new professional roles for teachers. ATLAS ideas are summed up in their section "The Development of Educators," using phrases such as "continuing high-quality education and development of adults" and "environments that sustain teacher engagement" to capture their approach (p. 21). CON used the term *learning community* to focus attention on the cluster concept in which teachers work collegially to promote their own development. CON also heavily emphasized teacher networks for further professional development (pp. 15–16).

ELOB put its ideas most elegantly in its proposal:

---

[9]MRSH design also talked about peer review, but only as a role for the master teachers—not as something undertaken by all teachers.

> Teachers are the lifeblood of any good school. Their professional development and renewal is crucial to the growth of student learning. The capacity of teachers to be lifelong learners is the mind spring of the high standards and *esprit de corps* without which school improvement is impossible. . . . Teachers themselves must be impelled into experiences for changes to happen in their teaching. An inner transformation must precede the outwardly visible improvements in the professional lives of teachers. . . . We have joined these elements in our design concept by changing the role of the teacher to expedition guide, reinforcing the teachers' responsibility for ongoing growth as a learner as well as the students in their charge. (p. 21)

These three designs envisioned much more teacher development of curriculum and instruction than the other three designs. They each saw teacher development and professionalization as the essence of the design. Some elements of the design were to be highly specified—ATLAS's governance structure, ELOB's multi-year looping, and CON's teacher clusters. These designs had more student-driven curriculum and instruction with the open-ended explorations of curriculum and essential questions. Consonant with that approach, the role of the teachers would necessarily change from deliverers of a predetermined curriculum to truly professional educators required to develop and use their expertise in developing their own curriculum and instruction, and they would do so through extensive teaming of teachers. Significant parts of the school day would be devoted to collegial interactions, and significant parts of the school year to professional development—not training.

Note that in addition to this role, each of these teams foresaw a significantly increased role for teachers in the governance structure of the schools or planning for school improvement. These three teams would help in this process by offering experiences and materials to enable growth. The teams wished to encourage the teachers to take on the responsibility for their own growth and for the school's improvement.

Intervening Experiences

The demonstration and scale-up phases experienced in the NAS partner districts were particularly harsh for the designs with school-based improvement approaches. As indicated above, the schools served under the district strategy were high-poverty, low-achieving schools in urban settings. The schools were concerned about reading and math score improvement, and they tended to have limited amounts of time for professional development given lack of resources or lack of control over existing resources (Bodilly, 1998).

Those designs that envisioned more expansive roles for teachers and that relied on having quality teachers to begin with—ones who could at least teach reading and math—were at a distinct disadvantage in the short term. In the meantime, a design like RW seemed well suited to these conditions because it could begin its training program to increase reading skills immediately. Others like MRSH and ATLAS would require a year of planning and working in committees before serious professional development addressing reading began. After a few months of experience, districts wondered if designs like ELOB and CON with the heavy emphasis on project-based instruction were well suited for elementary schools that needed quick improvements on reading test scores.

Design teams have spent the last several years realigning their teacher professionalization ideas to suit the needs of students and teachers in these schools. They have had to rethink how best to approach these schools both in terms of curriculum and instruction, which are already covered, and in terms of the most important professional development experiences to provide first. RW and AC have changed the least.

Several significant improvements came out of this adaptation. First, most teams now devote a significant portion of early professional development to school needs assessment. While using different processes, the purpose across designs is similar—to develop the capability of school staff to diagnose and understand their own successes and failures. Each design now includes this, but each in its own way.

This exercise is used by all designs as the basis for creating a long-term school-wide professional development plan. For example, review of data by committees of teachers in CON schools leads to a diagnosis of specific problems. Teachers and administrators then work to formulate a plan for school-wide professional development to address the issues. CON might supply some of this professional development, but some of it might come from other providers. The point is to have a long-term plan that helps address school-wide issues and not just the preferences of individual teachers. This school-wide plan, reducing individual teacher choice over professional development and forcing teachers to think in terms of school improvement, might now be the hallmark of an NAS design.

Second, by 1995 at the continued instigation of NAS and with new pressure from districts, teams began to consider the need for what became known as *benchmarks* (Bodilly, 1998). Benchmarks in this context are indicators of implementation keyed to the number of years of implementation a school had experienced. CON and NARE took the lead in this, but others followed. Soon design teams had constructed benchmarks to help schools and districts understand what implementation would look like—what was expected to be accomplished when. The benchmarks could also be used to judge the progress of an individual school compared to the norm.

Depending on how the team designed these benchmarks, they could become powerful mechanisms for professional development of teachers. Two contrasting approaches emerged along the lines already discussed. Those teams using design training approaches tended to develop benchmarks to be used by the design team representatives to assess the school's progress. Information would be fed back to the school. For example, RW used its implementation checklists and a follow-up written report to help inform the school of its progress toward implementation.

In contrast, those designs using a school-based professionalization approach took a different path. Their benchmarks were to be used by schools in a self-assessment process continuing the needs assessment process that took place in the first year of implementation. Often the benchmarks were set by the school using guidance from the teams. Schools would assess their own progress and make plans for improvement. In this assessment, consistent with the intent of these designs, the schools and teachers would take control of their own professional development. Teachers became the assessors and the peer reviewers—not the design team.

Third, several designs talked about the use of networks to further enhance professionalization of teachers (CON, ELOB, MRSH). CON had talked specifically about the importance of networks in its original proposal and developed a helpful, but also stressful, process called a Critical Friends visit. Teachers from CON schools across the country formed teams to visit other CON schools and review their progress toward adopting the design. In this formalized process, teachers acted as critics of other schools and formally evaluated their efforts. In interviews teachers rave about this experience—both those who have been the Critical Friends and those who have been the recipients of advice. These visits and summer workshops became the platform for teachers getting to know each other enough to begin exchanging e-mail and information with each other. As CON built its computer-based connections among schools, it provided chat rooms for teachers to exchange information, which was enabled by the contacts made through the Critical Friends process. Combined with the school-developed benchmarking process, CON has created tools for schools to use to help in the professionalization of its teachers.

The Critical Friends visits of CON can also be seen as a peer review process—in that particular case, school-to-school review. Other designs, especially ELOB, had talked about peer review as an important part of professional life that would lead to improved schools. Three designs, ATLAS, ELOB, and MRSH, have made substantial progress in developing the tools and/or processes under which this review occurs. Recall that these three designs plus CON required substantial development of units by teachers. Each set up their own processes for peer review of the units. MRSH does this through the central committee that plans and implements curriculum and instruction; nevertheless, teachers are still reviewing each other's work and providing feedback. ELOB accomplishes this through teacher group meetings and through display of teacher and student work called galleries. ATLAS uses its study groups of teachers as the basis for beginning peer review. Further development of the designs has led to more processes to encourage and even require peer review.

In at least one area, design teams had made little progress, and the current design descriptions show it. While not always stated bluntly, several designs assumed the school would have control over staffing, hiring, and firing as well as other incentives to promote professional development of teachers. Perhaps most important, one could infer from all the original proposals that teacher support for and implementation of the design elements would become a part of the normal teacher evaluations undertaken by schools. While the original designs did not talk about this, early conversations with teams indicated they thought this would eventually occur as part of the implementation process.

As with other elements already discussed, these powers and incentives remain largely controlled by the district and not the school. Schools undertaking a design usually only offer teachers recognition for their hard work at design implementation. Although that incentive remains powerful, other professional incentives can run counter to design implementation, for example, the monetary incentives offered to teachers for scoring well on standardized mandated tests.

Given control by the district it is no surprise that each district handles this in slightly different ways. Perhaps Memphis has been the most enlightened—it reviews the schools' design implementation as well as other standard indicators, and it holds principals and teachers accountable for giving the clear message that design implementation can lead to improved test scores. Still, the district controls the evaluation and incentive processes, not the school.

Professional Development as of 1998

While planned development has occurred, conflicts with local policy have forced adaptations. Most important, schools lacked the resources and control over professional development needed by designs; these are controlled by district policy. Design teams and their documents now take a more adaptive approach to these circumstances, leading to significant variation within a design team among schools in different locales.

- Most teams have adopted a needs assessment approach in the first year, dedicating some professional development resources to training teachers on how to assess the school's strengths and weaknesses and to develop a reasoned school improvement plan that coherently focuses professional development on solutions to identified problems.

- Several teams have worked to develop mechanisms for peer review.

- Most teams that required teachers to develop their own curriculum have found ways to ensure teachers share curriculum to avoid the need for so much individual curriculum writing.

- Several have developed mechanisms to increase networking among teachers across design schools.

- Significant differences exist among the teams with a split between those that focus on design training and those that focus on professionalization.

- Fundamental incentives for further professionalization of the staff and significant control over positions, hiring, firing, and bonuses are still not found in design-based schools and are not included in design documents. These elements are controlled by district and union policy.

Because of the differences among districts in the amount of funding available for implementation and the ability of the schools to control their budgets and scheduling, schools within a design team can show significant variation on this element.

NARE AS A COUNTEREXAMPLE

The discussion in this chapter has focused most closely on six teams: AC, ATLAS, CON, ELOB, MRSH, and RW. The seventh team that took part in the scale-up phase, NARE, did so under very different circumstances than the rest of the teams.

NARE is a very different design from the others. As explained in Chapter Two, NARE had its own district strategy—to work closely in partnership with several districts to change the environment in the districts and the schools as well. Aside from this difference, NARE was a standards-based design; it worked diligently with its partner, Learning Research and Development Center (University of Pittsburgh), to develop a set of standards for all grade levels for use in the NARE districts. While taking longer than expected, NARE produced and documented a set of standards, including performance standards, that have been impervious to criticism, and the districts accepted these standards. NARE also worked to develop an assessment system to go with the standards. Schools in these districts accepted the new ideas of NARE around embedded assessments but could not shake off the mandated state assessment systems.

NARE had five other elements: the learning environment, community services and supports, high performance, public engagement, and professional development. While its standards and assessment system developed and made progress in implementation, other elements of the design did not develop as expected or did not have the level of implementation impact the team desired. NARE did not have a prescriptive approach to curriculum, instruction, student grouping, and assignment elements. Like several other designs, it left the development of the learning environment to teachers based on their professional judgment and adoption of the NARE standards and assessment system. The design truly was standards-driven in the sense that it expected all other activities to flow from the adoption of the standards and assessment system. Its professional development element focused strongly on developing lead teachers and assumed that all teachers had the basic competence, time, and energy to translate the standards and assessment system into curriculum, instruction, and groupings. Its community involvement element was based on the Kentucky family support system model. The other important element of the design was its governance element: Schools were to have significant autonomy, but states and districts would adopt NARE standards, assessments, and teacher accountability elements.

From 1992 to 1997, NARE pursued these theories of education and change. Two findings from this period were clear, based on both RAND research and the team's own exposition of lessons learned. First, NARE never backed down from its theory of education. It made no accommodations or adaptations, rigidly adhering to the design principles. In point of fact, district and school personnel consistently complained about how difficult the team was to work with because it would not accommodate the school or district wishes, with this rigid adherence causing significant tensions between the design team and the partnering jurisdiction. Second, teachers in the schools reported they could not translate the NARE standards into curriculum and instruction without help. NARE was increasingly concerned that their stance on teacher-developed curriculum and instruction was not supportive of change. The team began to inquire about other approaches as early as 1997. It began to pursue connections to strong prescriptive curriculum developers, and the team explored better implementation assistance and support for schools.

In 1997, other factors proved important in bringing fundamental changes to the design. Most important was the federal government's work on developing the CSRD program, which clearly sent a signal to NARE that discretionary funding would be available at the school level. In contrast, NARE had always received its funding from districts. Another factor was that relationships in several of its districts deteriorated due to changes in superintendents or budget crises, threatening NARE's ability to make any further progress.

In part of 1997 and 1998 NARE retreated to rethink its theories of education and change and to learn from its own experiences and others. In 1998, the team emerged from this reflection with a new design called America's Choice. This design is still standards-based, using the standards and assessment developed previously, but, whereas once it dictated nothing about scheduling and instruction, it is now highly specified. For example, at the elementary level, it now is adamant about a block schedule with 2.5 hours for reading and literacy and a 1-hour math block. Like RW it provides a whole curriculum package aligned with its standards. The design has very specific parameters for governance, community involvement, and public engagement. The design areas have not changed, but their specificity has increased enormously. In addition, the implementation strategy changed to include much more whole-school training and exposure to design elements. Finally, while the design still maintained a district strategy, it allowed individual schools to join the team, while the team pressured the district for support. In short, the team sought multiple ways to ensure adoption and implementation.

With this new design, the team offered its services to new jurisdictions and the old partners. Some of the former partners declined in part because they could join only by committing to the new design. Others accepted, and new jurisdictions and schools joined.

The manner of change in this design is in sharp contrast to that of the others. While all teams experienced planned development, the NARE design did not experience slow district-by-district accommodation, adaptation, or drift, in part because it did not work under the same conditions as the other NAS designs. Rather its changes could be interpreted more as a complete reconcep-tualization given organizational learning or as a positive design adaptation. In contrast to other designs, the new America's Choice design applies equally to all new sites, without the variation by school seen in others. Rather than local adaptation, the team has seen fit to end partnerships. Rather than vagueness in certain areas, the design has grown significantly more specified and detailed.

IMPLICATIONS

Several different themes are evident in the changes made to the designs. The following findings are consonant with the literature that indicates that planned and unplanned adaptations would occur and that some of these adaptations would promote the design's concepts while others might retard it.

All designs have experienced planned development. Rhetorical arguments made in original proposals were converted over time to actual tools and processes for schools. Schools and teams developed significant amounts of curriculum and/or curricular units that could then be shared among new schools. Teams developed processes for better professional development of teachers. Teams also developed a process for cross-walking their standards to a district's standards. Teams developed diagnostic student assessments for teachers to use every day in the classroom that can lead students, teachers, and parents to a better understanding of student progress.

Interactions with teachers and students resulted in unplanned adaptations. The experiences of going to scale in poor urban districts led to significant changes within the designs. Student needs indicated the necessity of developing basic literacy and numeracy programs. Teacher needs promoted the development of rubrics for teachers to use for assessing student work against the district standards.

Lack of teacher will and capacity posed significant challenges to the concept of design-based assistance. In keeping with the implementation literature, one of the dominant reasons for some of the adaptations was lack of teacher time, motivation, or capacity. Design teams often found that teachers could not or would not develop curriculum and instructional materials. The teachers often claimed lack of time or capability. Teams found that so-called teacher leaders who received training did not go back to the school and train other teachers. Thus, some designs never really penetrated past a shallow implementation to be able to test if the design really had effects on teachers and students. This lack was abetted by district policies that did not provide resources for teacher time, joint or common planning time, or that did not award teachers for unit development. It was also abetted by design team assumptions about the capability of teachers especially in the areas of math, science, and curriculum development and the inability of some teams to provide clear instructions and useful guidelines to teachers.

If teachers are unable to take on these tasks successfully, then only those efforts that bring embedded knowledge and time will be tenable. Several of the teams such as RW and now America's Choice have produced extensive materials that embed design concepts such as fully articulated standards and curriculum and have had some significant success in the marketplace in terms of number of school adoptions.

A caveat on this finding is necessary. We examined implementation only in the scale-up sites and these sites had peculiar characteristics, and several of the teams had only very limited experiences outside of these sites. Therefore, this finding might be limited to urban districts, often beset by budget difficulties, largely serving students from impoverished families.

Interactions with existing policy environments resulted in further unplanned adaptations. Most designs now adopt district standards or provide a cross-walking to show that their standards do not conflict with those of the district. They all accept mandated assessments even if they conflict with design notions. They all allow the adoption of mandated curriculum by the district, even if it conflicts with their proposed scope and sequence. With the exception of NARE, design teams have either accepted mandated district literacy and math skills programs, developed their own, or adopted existing ones as their own. In addition, most design teams have backed away from aggressive statements for immediate concessions to schools concerning school self-governance. Instead, the designs often encourage a process by which schools can slowly work toward more self-governance. Finally, with the exception of NARE, designs that had high hopes for integrated social services take a more opportunistic approach—promoting integration when the district and local providers are ready. Meanwhile, they have developed school-level approaches that help meet at least part of the vision. The bottom line is that the practical reality of working with these districts has driven design teams to lengthen implementation schedules, drop elements, or advocate principles to be worked toward rather than established up front.

Adaptation has led to extensive local variation within designs and potential incoherence with schools. The accommodating stance taken by most designs in their newer versions of design documents allows significant variation in sites associated with a single team. This accommodation is in keeping with the general approach originally outlined in the NAS proposal for "designs to be adaptable so that they can be used by many communities" (NASDC, 1991, p. 21). In this sense adaptability to local circumstances can be seen in a positive light. On the other hand, the more local variation not only occurs but is encouraged, the more the edges blur between a design-based school and a school generally attempting to improve itself using an external provider of training.

In addition, this variation not only allows but promotes incoherence and fragmentation within the school—the antithesis of the original intention of the NAS design concept. NAS schools based on several of the current design documents could potentially have district-mandated standards, a conflicting set of assessments, and a combination of district-mandated and design-promoted curriculum and instruction, with no changes expected in governance or social services beyond some design-dictated committees. When teams allow mandated standards, assessment, and curriculum to substitute for their own, the design's coherence is lessened, as is the possibility of ever reaching the full vision of the design. Within this study the NARE and RW designs stand in contrast to the others, promoting less variation or accommodation to their design specifications.

This phenomenon of drift from the original intentions of the RFP cannot be labeled as poor implementation.   Current design documents and actual implementation by several teams allow this drift to occur. It is not surprising then that teachers in design-based schools in some districts report that they do not understand the design, that the district is not supportive of the design, or that they no longer choose to pursue the design because it does not fit where the district is now going (Bodilly, 1998; Berends et al., 2000).

Discussions in NAS conferences now reflect growing concern over what it terms quality control. As the designs adapt to fit new circumstances, this issue of quality control continues to surface. NAS and teams continually asked, " what is the essence of the design and who decides this?" If the state, district, or union is the decisionmaker, then design coherence is likely to suffer and NAS and design teams cannot claim to provide coherent designs.

Significant differences among designs still remain. Significant differences in approach were evident from the very beginning. Discussion at NAS often categorized these as differences between product designs (AC and RW) and process designs (ATLAS, CON, ELOB, MRSH, NARE) or as more or less prescriptive. The product designs tended to and still have design team–developed or –delivered curriculum and instructional scope and sequence, content, or actual units; professional development geared toward design implementation; and less emphasis on governance issues. The process designs were from the very beginning less interested in specifying what teachers were to do and more interested in helping teachers and schools through a process of growth, renewal, and improvement.   They had more teacher-developed curriculum approaches, more changes to governance, and more long-term professional development concepts.

Experiences in implementation have led to a blurring of some of these distinctions. For example, with the exception of ELOB, all designs now have some fundamental reading programs whether they are those mandated by the district, newly created by the team, or swiftly adopted from an existing program. In addition, changes to designs have led CON and MRSH to hold some middle ground between these other two groupings of designs. While CON remains process oriented in its curriculum and professional development, it retracted from the governance changes originally advocated. At the same time, it has developed very specific process structures to guide teachers and schools in their improvement path. Thus, while still process oriented, it has a highly specified process. MRSH firmly maintains a foot in both worlds with some significant portions of curriculum provided by the design, but some provided by teachers. Certainly the NARE design, as reconceptualized, has become much more specified and prescriptive.

Given these adaptations, it is difficult to assess if the designs are effective in producing improved student outcomes. The designs have changed significantly and in general have not been implemented to such a degree that they would be expected to have strong effects (Bodilly, 1998; Berends, et al., 2000). Perhaps more important, some designs now allow so much variation that it is hard to ascribe the design as a cause of any student effects.

Although it is reasonable to hypothesize that the design adaptation has so diluted the original interventions that few effects can be associated with the original design concept—that has not yet been proven. What can be said is that design adaptation has allowed enough incoherence and fragmentation to persist in supposedly design-based schools that any measurement of student achievement would not be measuring the effect of the concept of a coherent design. It could, however, be measuring the effect of design team assistance to schools: the professional development and additional resources accorded to these schools.

Chapter Four

DEVELOPMENT OF IMPLEMENTATION STRATEGIES AND SUPPORTS

This chapter addresses the changes over the past several years in the implementation strategies and support adopted by the different designs to enable schools to fully implement their designs. The original RFP outlined seven proposal requirements. Somewhat aware of the importance of implementation support, NAS required attention to implementation strategies:

> Explain how you will persuade others to put your design in place. . . . Bidders will be expected to demonstrate their understanding of the complexities of implementing their design, outline initial strategies for proceeding, and provide at least a general idea of how they plan to encourage adaptation and use of the design following initial testing and implementation. (NASDC, 1991, p. 25)

In general it can be said that the original designs had some broad ideas about how to approach implementation but had few specific practices developed (Bodilly et al., 1996; Bodilly, 1998). Teams had small proposal sections devoted to implementation usually outlining their partner sites, but most teams concentrated on describing the elements of their design.[1] While the discussions of implementation

---

[1]The one exception was NARE, which specified that no school could sustain a design on its own and must be supported by a district. This team included a district and state change strategy not seen in other designs, which set the NARE design apart from the very beginning. The other designs focused on schools with perhaps one exception— ATLAS; its pathway strategy required autonomy for a feeder pattern of schools within a district.

were not extensive, failure to address it at all led to disqualification of a proposal.

Two themes were common across designs in terms of broad conceptions about how to approach implementation. Reflecting lessons from previous implementation experience, most teams wanted teacher involvement in the process of selecting a design and implementing it (McLaughlin, 1990). They wanted to avoid a top-down process of implementation that was bound to fail (Usdan, 1994; Schwarz, 1994). To encourage teacher involvement, some teams asked for teacher voting to approve the selection of the design or at least a process of consensus. ATLAS, CON, and MRSH proposed teacher task forces or committees to develop the design practices within the school. NARE asked for incentives for performance, teacher teams, and leadership training for teachers.

The other fairly common concept was that schools should take part in a needs or strengths assessment fairly early in the implementation process. Just what that meant was not well developed in the proposals, but it was evident. AC defined an assessment of community assets that could be used for the constructive actions of the students and for speakers in the classrooms. The MRSH and NARE designs called for a more formal school assessment that would be the work of school-level committees in the first year.

Over the past several years, implementation strategies and supports have emerged and developed. Like the other elements of the designs, implementation strategies show interesting contrasts in philosophy and core beliefs.

These changes are in part due to the changing nature of the relationship between design teams and NAS. The relationship started with significant funding awards for provocative ideas not always based in practical application. The teams, largely composed of developers and people with interesting ideas, were recipients of these funds and used them for the development and testing of ideas. Over time, the NAS scale-up strategy has driven home the need for implementation strategies and supports. In response the teams have evolved into service organizations facing real market challenges in their pursuit of increasing numbers of client schools.

In addition, the market for the teams' product changed. Promoting transformation in a handful of schools is one thing—it is quite another across 50, 60, or even hundreds of schools. NAS's push to "go to scale" or increase the volume of customers had an impact on what the design teams could offer in terms of assistance and still remain self-sustaining. This new fact of life for teams had important implications. For example, prior to this teams could work very intensively with a handful of schools—transmitting their ideas and knowledge person to person. With the move to scale, teams were forced to rely more heavily on printed word, video, conferencing, etc., as the means to transfer the design principles to the school, which required greater clarity and a greater articulation of design concepts.

The result has been a major shift for most of the teams. The original proposals focused very closely on the actual design elements, and the teams were largely made up of curriculum developers, assessment experts, etc. Teams still have some portion of their staff devoted to further development, but a greater portion of staff is devoted to implementation—selecting new schools, training teachers, or training trainers. Teams are no longer primarily design-developing organizations; they are now primarily assistance organizations. This is not to say that the teams no longer develop their designs—several have set aside resources for further development. For example, ELOB still devotes 10 percent of its funds to development each year. NARE and RW have received grants from the Department of Education to further develop their middle school and high school concepts. In general, however, funding for further development has dwindled compared to earlier years.

This chapter describes the development of the implementation process, separate from the design elements. Four areas of the process are discussed in turn. While these areas do not fully represent all the changes, they represent major developments in the implementation strategies of designs and are consistent with the expectations laid out in the literature review.

Gaining support from school staff is an essential first step in ensuring implementation; therefore, the first section describes the development of a school selection process. Several teams asserted that the development of a "community of practice" at the school level is essential to progress toward and sustainment of long-term changes to the behaviors implemented. Thus, the chapter covers the development of the concept of promoting a community of practice. The development of strong assistance packages required for implementation is covered in the third section. Finally, the chapter describes the means by which design teams maintain quality control—the central issue of fidelity that plagues all reform efforts.

THE SCHOOL MATCHING OR SELECTION PROCESS

McLaughlin (1990) in revisiting the original RAND Change Agent study questioned the original finding that practice would follow belief. In other words, school staff would have to voluntarily undertake the reform and be intellectually supportive of it before they would adopt the practices of the reform. Other research supports McLaughlin's original view—that mandates often fail because those who implement them do not buy into reforms adequately to motivate their energy toward reform (Bardach, 1977; Mazmanian and Sabatier, 1989; Weatherley and Lipsky, 1977). McLaughlin does not disagree completely but notes that in some cases mandated reforms have been implemented and that belief followed the adoption of practice.

If one thing has been learned through the NAS initiative, it is that the introduction of schools to design teams is important to ultimate implementation (Stringfield and Datnow, 1998; Bodilly, 1998; Wong and Meyer, 1998). Failure to enter the school in a positive light often permanently prejudiced the design team's efforts in that school. Not only is it important to screen possible candidate schools carefully, but the selection process itself is crucial in developing the trust and enthusiasm necessary to sustain design implementation. These important lessons were often learned the hard way—through bad experiences.

Selection in the Original Proposals

At the time of the original proposals, three of the designs had already chosen or partnered with schools, districts, or states with whom they intended to more fully develop the design and demonstrate it. The others had received letters of interest or were beginning discussions with particular schools and districts.[2]

By the demonstration phase each had selected partner schools for the two-year period in which the teams would demonstrate their designs in real settings. As indicated in other documents (Bodilly et al., 1996; Glennan, 1998), these schools were chosen primarily based on the original partnerships and personal relationships. For the most part, the schools that partnered with designs in this period received low cost or free services or materials from the teams—a flow-through of the NAS funding for teams. Some schools were more fortunate and received significant capital in the form of computer equipment or other technology. During this phase, resources and the pressing need for results drove the selection without much thought as to what would occur during scale-up. The exception was NARE, which fully intended to scale up within its jurisdiction partners.

In reality, little about this initial experience would prepare design teams for a careful selection process for scale-up.[3] Most importantly,

---

[2]AC: Partnership discussions under way in seven schools, one in each of the following areas: San Diego, Mississippi, Chicago, Phoenix, Rhode Island, Washington, D.C., New York City.

ATLAS: Expression of interest from 60 schools in 17 states.

CON: Partners with two schools: Sarah Greenwood School, Boston; Woodland Street School, Worcester.

ELOB: Expression of interest from three to five school systems involved in Outward Bound programs.

MRSH: Expression of interest from seven different districts.

NARE: Partnerships with Arkansas, Kentucky, New York, Vermont, Washington, Pittsburgh, Rochester, San Diego, White Plains.

RW: Partners with four schools in one school district in St. Mary's County, Md.

[3]See Bodilly, 1998. Review of the original design documents shows only two teams wrote about the selection process during scale-up: NARE and RW. Several other teams did discuss briefly what they would offer to new schools—videotapes, training, materials—but did not discuss how they would acquire new schools. RW said it expected to replicate in eight sites, if need be, through advertisements. The team would visit schools that had expressed letters of interest to explain the program and show videotapes. After a few weeks of discussion and debate "school staff would vote as to whether or not they wish to participate. Only schools in which at least 80% agree will be selected" (p. 31). After the school facilitators and a family support person were selected for the new schools, they would travel to the St. Mary's sites and spend two

there was little connection because scale-up would entail charging schools for services and working in large districts attempting to encourage systemic changes in district policy—something not attempted in the demonstration phase.

Intervening Experiences

As the design teams navigated the hurdles of the demonstration phase, NAS began to push them to think about the scale-up phase and how schools would be chosen, especially in the NAS partner districts (NARE districts were less involved in this discussion). At design team conferences several different issues were raised and discussed but often not resolved:

- **Was there a single set of criteria that design teams could use to screen schools to identify a good match?** The design teams did not agree on these criteria and little was done to explore this issue more systematically or analytically.

- **How much effort and how many resources should be put into marketing to get a good match versus actual delivery of assistance?** As teams began their own expansions during demonstration, they began to understand the costs associated with extensive hand-holding and preselection visits to schools. Costs per actual match were high with some teams such as ATLAS, ELOB, and CON. A design like ATLAS required extensive discussions at the district level to set up the concept of a pathway, a labor-intensive process with high costs per school selected. In contrast, the RW design had extensive experience with this issue given its Success for All program: It sent out free materials and brochures to hundreds of schools explaining the design. Demand was high enough and its brand name recognizable enough that it could pick and choose among applications given this low-cost marketing.

- **Should schools be given a choice as to whether or not to go with a design?** Most teams agreed that schools should be given a choice as to which team to select. RW was adamant that this be

---

weeks in training and observation of the programs. NARE intended to replicate within the partner or member jurisdictions.

an anonymous vote with an 80 percent approval rate. Others were not so formal, arguing more for a consensus building process and approval by the principal or school improvement team. Others such as ATLAS and MRSH had argued for a more prolonged process. Both of these teams thought that an initial agreement to work with a school could be reached by negotiation with just the principal or school improvement team. The team would then work with the school for a year. At that point the full faculty would vote for continuing or not.

By 1995, NAS began to be more of a player in how schools would select teams—at least within the NAS partner districts—and proposed a selection process for the scale-up partner districts. Ideally, it would start with schools attending a design team fair where schools could wander from booth to booth or room to room to pick up materials and listen to descriptions or videos on each team including those not under the NAS umbrella. School representatives would review the materials and pick one or two teams of particular interest. These teams would then visit the interested school and the interested school could send representatives to a school actually implementing the designs (McLaughlin, 1990, covers why this step is so important). Finally, a vote of the full staff would take place, with a clear majority needed to proceed.

Districts, however, interceded in this process. For the most part, NAS partner districts mandated that schools adopt designs. Thus, while schools might be able to choose among designs, they did not feel they could refuse to adopt any design. Some districts, such as Cincinnati, prescreened designs and did not allow certain designs to work in the district. Other districts molded the design fair process more to their liking. Some, such as Dade and Memphis, working in conjunction with the local teachers union, created their own rules for voting or teacher participation. Finally, some districts, such as Cincinnati, took a strong hand in matching schools to designs using their own knowledge of what might work. Thus, school personnel often reported that they did not have a free choice in the selection of a design (Bodilly, 1998; Berends et al., 2000). As one teacher described the voting process, "we voted until we got it right."

In non-NAS districts, teams were free to pursue their own methods of marketing and selection and considerable variation was evident. RW kept to a hands-off process of sending materials and letting schools follow up. ATLAS, CON, and ELOB had a much more labor-intensive process; ELOB in particular relied heavily on personal interactions and networks to develop new sites.

In the NARE districts, a different process was used, developed by NARE. This process often involved a competition with RFPs to schools to apply to the design team and for funding from the district for the services of the team.

One district policy served the purposes of the design teams well. In schools that really did positively vote to implement the design, some teachers might still have been opposed to the design. In several districts, especially Memphis, these teachers were initially allowed to transfer to another school, thus not blocking the implementation of the design. This process worked well for teams, as none of them ever achieved 100 percent approval. Without this type of policy, design teams ran the risk of their efforts being undermined by disgruntled teachers who did not support the initial vote. Several design teams did experience at least one or two implementation failures in the scale-up phase because of a strong backlash to the selection process, or lack thereof, by teachers who did not subsequently leave the school.

From all these different interactions, teams drew several lessons (Bodilly, 1998; Berends, et al., 2000):

- Design teams needed to improve their descriptive materials to quickly convey the nature of the design.

- Design teams needed to convey the types of work that the school would undertake in adopting the design, the training requirement, or requirements, for teachers to develop curriculum.

- Design teams needed a clear and consistent cost structure to enable districts or schools to make reasonable choices grounded in affordability.

- School choice was important, and all designs needed to encourage informed and free decisionmaking by the school personnel.

• Design teams needed to reduce the cost of this process while making it effective.

All of these lessons implied a greater reliance on clear printed materials and communication processes that reduced belabored interactions between the team and the school. They also implied the need for some firmness in the negotiation process. For example, some design teams had originally been very unsure of their costs and allowed for significant negotiation over what would be provided. Thus, costs of a design could vary significantly from district to district. RW and NARE seemed to be the exceptions to this; they had identified a very specific and fairly nonnegotiable price structure before the scale-up phase. After these initial experiences in scale-up, all the teams agreed they should develop a firm price structure.

Over the course of several years, design teams have developed materials that describe their designs: brochures, pamphlets, videos, and Web sites. These help schools understand the nature of the design and also describe the nature of the matching process to be used. For example, MRSH now has a package of materials that includes one-pagers on the design team organization, training, sites, consultants, staff, design overview, essential elements, evidence of success, and next steps. Next steps include the statements: "Unless otherwise negotiated with your district, MRSH requires evidence that eighty percent of the teachers at a proposed site have voted by secret ballot to join the MRSH initiative."

RW has developed a package of materials that includes descriptions of the design, news releases about the design, estimated costs, a pamphlet on "Considerations for Adoption," and another called "Steps to Becoming a Roots and Wings School."

While the brochures and pamphlets are clearly meant for marketing, they also contain important information about the conditions under which designs can flourish in schools. More and more they provide information to the schools that help them better pick and choose among designs based on conditions in their community and schools. The information can be as simple as making sure schools understand the RW design will not prosper in a school that does not commit to a full-time facilitator and a full-time family support person. Or it can help schools understand whether the curriculum and instructional materials will come to them fully developed as with AC, NARE, and RW or must be partially developed by the school and staff as with ATLAS, CON, ELOB, and MRSH.

Summary of Selection Process Development

Selection was not a real issue until the scale-up phase. Experiences helped identify the selection process as an important part of the assistance in the design-based assistance package offered by NAS teams and the experiences in schools. In particular the needs of teachers and others for clearer and more detailed descriptions of design and the work of implementation drove the teams toward more specific materials and development of selection processes. These changes can be seen as either: (1) adaptations due to client needs; or (2) further design development based on newly identified needs. However, one would not put the adjective *planned* in front of that development. Scale-up experiences led to the recognition of the importance for further work on the selection process.

All design teams have developed promotional materials to describe their designs to school-level decisionmakers. While differences exist in the processes (from district to district as well as from team to team when working independently), a principle has emerged. Schools must have informed and free decisionmaking when considering a design, and schools should be informed of the conditions under which the design will work. All the design team materials and processes developed have this end in mind. In addition, teams have developed processes that reduce the costs of marketing for the team, relying more heavily over time on printed and other materials rather than personal contact.

Finally, given the implementation failures in several schools due to lack of teacher buy-in, the teams are more likely to turn down matches that seem ill-advised from the start, especially ones where a group of teachers is adamantly opposed to a design. The lesson here is that an 80 percent approval in a vote is meaningless if the 20 percent who are against the adoption of the design are adamantly opposed to it. NAS also supports teachers being able to transfer out of design-based schools if those teachers do not support the design.

COMMUNITY OF TEACHERS

Another important part of most teams' implementation strategies is creating a community of learners that will work toward school improvement using the design. While some teams, such as ATLAS and the original NARE designs, mean a larger community, most teams focused on the community of teachers within the school who would effectively work together as colleagues to further develop and enhance the design in the school over the long term. This notion is similar to that proposed by other authors (Mohrman, Lawler, and Mohrman, 1992; Warren Little, 1990, 1982; Rosenholtz, 1990)—it assumes that a prescribed curriculum and instructional package will not survive long in a school. It emphasizes the importance of teachers working collegially over a long period of time to develop a culture of innovative practice that would further develop and extend the design in a local adaptation.

For several teams the idea of developing a community of teachers working toward improvement over time was more important than the selection process. For example, for specified designs such as AC or RW, learning about the design and choosing it in an informed way was heavily emphasized as the cornerstone of the process of building a community. For other designs, such as ATLAS, CON, ELOB, MRSH, and NARE, the selection process was not as important, at least originally, as the process of community building that came after a choice of designs. This explains why ATLAS and MRSH had initially wanted schools to have a second chance to "vote" or approve the design a year after the initial selection.

Thus, these designs, (ATLAS, CON, ELOB, MRSH, NARE) set up committee structures and task forces as the means by which teachers would learn and actually develop the design within the school. Note these designs tended to be less specified than the AC and RW design. The work of the committees was actually to develop the specifics of the design within the school.

ATLAS and NARE were especially concerned about the development of leaders within the school, other than just the principal. The heads of their respective committees and task forces were provided with opportunities for more extensive training and development. For these two designs, in particular, the "train the trainer" model was adopted in part because of this leadership concept. Lead teachers would receive design team training and then help other teachers in the school to understand the design, begin to incorporate it into their committee or task force work, and finally infuse it into their everyday practice. Another reason for this training approach was cost. These two teams did not believe that they could afford to train all teachers within a school and still expand as NAS wanted. For them, extensive whole-school training such as provided by RW was out of the question.

A major finding of past NAS studies by RAND (Bodilly, 1998) was that this "train the leader" model did not work well to change curriculum and instruction in the school building—at least in the time period observed. Given the extent of curriculum change demanded, teams that emphasized whole-school training and extensive written materials and support had seemingly more short-term success in implementing curriculum and instructional elements.

Yet, the lead-teacher approach did serve in several instances to extend the leadership of the school in important ways. Several schools in the scale-up phase reported growth in the capacity and knowledge of their leadership teams and in the school capacity to respond to new initiatives due to this training; this finding was especially prevalent in NARE sites in Kentucky and Washington state.

As in other areas, NARE provided a different approach to this whole issue. Initially in the scale-up phase it established that each district that worked with it would get a fixed number of professional development days from NARE, in the form of experts NARE would send to the site. The district itself would be responsible for selecting a local "design team," a group of district administrators who would be responsible for ensuring the design was understood and implemented by the schools. This local design team would be provided with extensive training by NARE and then would offer its services to the school-level teams consisting of the heads of the different task forces that NARE required within the school to work on the key areas of the design: learning environments, standards and assessments, public engagement, etc.

In the RAND evaluation of the scale-up phase, teachers reported that the NARE system worked well when districts provided for full-time personnel in these assignments and considerable professional development days for all the teachers (Bodily, 1998). It did not work well when these conditions were not met.

In its new incarnation as America's Choice, NARE still includes these notions of task force leadership, but it does emphasize more direct aid to teachers in terms of predeveloped curriculum and training specific to that curriculum. ATLAS has dropped many different committees but has developed one firm rule: All teachers will participate in teacher study groups in the first several years of scale-up. They might not join other committees but they will be part of the study groups that work within and between schools.

Other teams learned similar important lessons from the experience and adapted their strategy accordingly. As these designs have evolved, so have the committee structures and training associated with them. The specific committees required have changed names and/or some of their functions. For each of these designs the importance of the committees, grade-level meetings, or common planning time in the further development of the design or in the development of the community of learners has not lessened. This part of the strategy has remained constant, and design teams still search for ways to improve and maintain teacher interactions in support of a collegial environment.

As indicated in the next section, several now provide very mixed professional development offerings for teachers—emphasizing whole-school and committee or leadership training. Each team has looked for ways to ensure that a community of learners develops—whether through mandated committee structures, required grade-level planning, the use of houses as an organizing mechanism, or implementation review processes. All teams report struggling to more diligently address the need to develop leadership within the schools, although it is not always clear what answers they have implemented.

ASSISTANCE TO SCHOOLS

As noted above, the original designs lacked much detail on how they would assist schools in implementing the design, yet the literature indicates that without this important support the designs would not take hold. The scale-up phase saw a burgeoning of activity in the area. New pamphlets and brochures can help explain the design quickly to possible new sites. The core of design-based assistance is more extensive: materials that describe standards, curriculum, instruction, professional development, etc.; the training and professional development provided by teams; networks with other teachers; and other supports provided by teams. Given these items simply did not exist at the proposal stage, we describe the lessons that emerged from the intervening experience and attempt to explain several patterns evident in the current assistance packages.

Lessons from the Intervening Years

Other RAND reports have documented several lessons (Bodilly et al., 1996; Bodilly, 1998; Glennan, 1998; Berends, et al., 2000) that align well with other research views of the need for implementation assistance and support (McLaughlin, 1990; Bikson and Eveland, 1989; Eveland and Bikson, 1992; Bikson et al., 1997; Bikson and Eveland, 1998; Mazmanian and Sabatier, 1989). These are:

- Teachers need materials to understand what they are supposed to teach and how they are supposed to teach it—the more detailed and specific the better. For product designs this meant the actual curriculum to use. For process designs this meant exemplary units and a detailed process to guide teachers through development.

- Teachers need someone they can turn to with questions—the more accessible the better. This assistance could be design team hot lines, chat rooms, actual facilitators at the school level, or frequent visits by the team.

- While helping teachers with curriculum and instruction was key, schools also needed help in establishing some basic school improvement processes. These might include training in new governance structures, leadership development, school improvement planning, and site-based budgeting.

- Because teachers would prefer more hands-on assistance, design teams needed to develop the means to provide assistance within cost constraints. The more labor-intensive processes used in early implementation could not be sustained in scale-up.

- Limits on professional development days were imposed by districts and the resources they made available. In addition, professional development days were constrained by teacher and parent concerns about having too many substitutes during the course of the school year.

- Limits on teacher time for sharing, either imposed by schedules or by teachers themselves, slowed implementation as did excessive turnover of teachers in some schools. Both led to the inability to support the learning time needed by teachers to adopt designs and extend them deeply into the school.

- Training the lead teachers to train other staff did not have strong support in schools. Lead teachers who went to conferences often did not bring information of value back to those who did not attend. Design teams began to focus more on whole-school training and to develop more complex training programs varying whole-staff training with small-group or individual training.

- Districts demanded that design teams provide some sort of liaison to the district and schools. Districts wanted on-site personnel to address their questions and concerns as well.

In response to these identified needs or concerns, the teams offered the training listed in Table 4.1.

Development of Materials. All designs have undertaken serious material development from better initial descriptions of their programs to more fully articulated exemplary curriculum units. These materials manifest themselves in different ways. For example, 1,600 or more hours of curriculum were developed by Roots and Wings, extensive units were developed by ELOB teachers throughout the country, and AC developed a curriculum planner. In addition, the NARE design developed from few such materials, other than its extensive standards and assessments, to a full curriculum and instructional package to aid teachers in ensuring the curriculum and instruction will help students meet the high standards proposed.

Use of Facilitators. Originally only two teams required the use of school-level facilitators, AC and RW. These facilitators are personnel chosen by the school, trained by the design team, and work on-site to help answer teachers' questions, coach teachers, ensure the design is implemented, and distribute the needed materials. In the intervening years, CON added this position as a part of its design.

In addition, work with districts usually indicated that a district facilitator was useful once a team had a cluster of schools working with a district. NARE used this approach all during the demonstration phase and scale-up. This approach now has been adopted by CON, ELOB, MRSH, and RW, and each of these teams provides district-level facilitators or coordinators. In some cases the district shares the cost of this person, in other cases the district pays the full cost (such as NARE), and in other cases the design has taken up this cost.

Other Positions. RW and CON also had required additional positions. For RW this position is the family support coordinator, which remains a part of the design. CON at one time required a technology coordinator in the school; although no longer required, it is often adopted.

Training Format and Quantity. Original proposals varied in the amount of time required for teacher development. For example, ELOB said it would require 20 days of professional development per year, which was not just for training in the design, but was in keeping with its ideas of collegiality and professional development overall. On the other hand, AC sought only five days of training dedicated to the design in the initial year. In addition, several teams provided only leadership training. Selected teachers and the principal would receive training and in turn train the other teachers.

Table 4.1 shows the 1998 structure as we understand it. Some teams (AC, MRSH) are very specific about the types and amounts of training provided; others such as ATLAS are less so. Some fall in between— CON, ELOB, and RW provide general notions, but allow schools some choices depending upon local circumstances.

The amount of training provided varies considerably. AC provides the least number of days and does so primarily in the first year; assistance in the remaining years is largely implementation checks, not training. In contrast, ELOB requires 20 days per teacher per year and this lasts for three years. The actual amount of training for a given design varies significantly by district depending on district policy.

The format of training varies. AC offers only whole-staff training; others offer more variety, with ELOB offering a significant menu of options.

Table 4.1

Design Team Training Offerings as of 1998

	AC	ATLAS	CON	ELOB	MRSH	RW
Training grouping and days[a] in first year						
Whole staff	5	2–3 times per year	3	√	12	3
Principal		3–6	3	√	4	5
Leadership team		4	√	√	4	√
Facilitator/ other	√		10			5
Selected individual/ small groups		√		√	11	6
Conference		√	3 person/3 day	√	√	2 person/ 3 days
Negotiable additional training		Yes, not specified	Yes, determined in bench-marking process	20–40 days/ teacher in any of the above		23 days on-site assistance total
New position						
School facilitator	√		√			√
Regional facilitator	√	√	√	√	√	
Other						√

[a]Numbers are specified when provided; √ means that type of training is provided but numbers of days are not specified.

Turnover. One problem not addressed above is excessive turnover of teachers in some schools. In some schools, this turnover amounted to 25 to 33 percent of the teacher force on a yearly basis. District policies or the school environment prompted the turnover—it was not a result of adopting the design. This turnover created a continuing demand for design-based assistance, one that few teams were able to sustain. Given limited commitment of funds and unlimited demands for assistance, some schools were simply unable to keep up. Design teams grew increasingly aware of this problem and have sought solutions such as the train the trainer mode. But the real solution lies in district policies that are outside the control of teams.

Summary of Development of Design-Based Assistance Concept

RAND has already written extensively about the development of the design-based assistance concept, noting that the concept is not new.

> Many organizations provide assistance in the context of a design. In most cases this assistance relates to assistance in a single program, perhaps in reading, math, or science. . . . The distinguishing feature of the NAS initiative is that it has deliberately set out to develop a variety of design-based assistance organizations with which schools can choose to affiliate. It has invested not only in creating the designs themselves but also in developing organizations and their strategies for engaging and assisting schools to implement their designs. (Glennan, 1998, p. 22)

The factors driving this development are several: limited planned development, a great deal of adaptation to the needs of the teachers as clients, and some adaptations to conflicting policy. The middle factor is by far the most important in understanding this growth in development. The assistance packages continue to develop as designs gain experience with different districts. These packages have grown from virtually nothing to a set of clearer design descriptions; a set of benchmarks for the designs; a full array of curriculum and instruction material for designs such as RW and America's Choice; conference offerings; professional development/training; and other services. These developed packages have been molded in turn by the needs of the particular districts and clients served with emphasis on needs assessments and some basic skills emerging as important. Even with this growth, some schools with significant teacher turnover demand more assistance than can reasonably be provided.

MAINTAINING QUALITY

In discussions with teams a major challenge over the years has been how to maintain the quality of implementation so as to affect student performance. We think of these generally as quality assurance or quality control issues. These issues were addressed in the original RFP; in the outline of expected topics against which proposals would be judged, one of the seven topics addressed quality control:

> Define how you (and NASDC) will know if it works. NASDC will be concerned with the quality of the bidder's plans for self-assessment. The design effort must be outcome-oriented and the design teams are expected to establish benchmark measures by which they will assess their process toward those outcomes. (NASDC, 1991, p. 24)

The original RFP demanded that teams provide for their own continued self-assessment.

> Credible self-assessments by design teams will be important to NASDC's monitoring of design efforts and to providing information to communities that contemplate implementing the design. NASDC will also sponsor continuing independent assessment of the team's progress. (NASDC, 1991, p. 35)

On the edges, evaluation of student outcomes in implementing schools can conflate with design teams' need for self-assessment. Both require two types of data: (1) knowledge of what was or was not implemented or what occurred in the school that might have caused an effect, and (2) knowledge of student outcomes. One purpose for analyzing these data is strictly evaluative on behalf of customers: the school, the district, funders, or the public. Another, and the one at the heart of this discussion, is to help a design team understand if the design implementation is leading to desirable outcomes and, if not, what needs to be improved to get those outcomes: the design or the assistance package.

Early during the demonstration phase, RAND asked each design team an important question, "How will we know if the design is being implemented?" The answer was often obscure as the designs were still in a rapid stage of development, and reliance on fidelity to written proposals would give a misleading picture of the implementation. Thus, RAND developed its own indicators of design implementation. During the scale-up phase, the superintendent of the Memphis City school district asked NAS, "How will we know if the designs are being implemented?" Other districts also began to ask. At the same time, as part of its analytic support, RAND asked the design teams the same question adding the need to distinguish between first-year implementation, second-year implementation, and so on.

Starting with very little in the way of specifics, the design teams have attempted to address this issue, with one major exception. The following paragraphs explain some of the means by which teams have begun to assess and assure quality.

Benchmarks for Implementation and Implementation Checks

As a result of the queries by districts and others, the design teams began to develop what became known as benchmarks for implementation. While this term was originally used in the RFP, the concept behind it was unclear, and the need for benchmarks actually had become lost during the demonstration phase. Queries from schools and districts reminded NAS and its teams of this need.

Design teams, if they had not already, began the development of benchmarks. The first draft of benchmarks for each team was given to Memphis for use by the University of Memphis in assessing the level of implementation in schools. The University of Memphis took these drafts and developed its own set of benchmarks. Meanwhile, the design teams tested and further developed their own benchmarks.

The end result of the design teams' efforts is a document by each design team that describes both the activities that a school would undertake during each year of implementation and the means by which it would be evident that the school had accomplished that activity. These benchmarks have become the cornerstone of the assistance package provided to schools. Specifically, design teams have more adeptly identified and described core practices and have translated these practices into benchmarks for schools to understand the goals and sequence of implementation. More than any other assistance offered, they clearly delineate each design teams' expectations.

For example, the ATLAS benchmarks include objectives, strategies, and accomplishments in five different areas. The accomplishments or benchmarks for early implementation of teaching and learning components include:

- Different learning styles that are acknowledged and accommodated
- Standards-associated frameworks and curriculum that are in place and that articulate within grade and across grade expectations
- Essential questions that are posted in the classroom.

Further experience with the design should lead to further accomplishments such as:

- Implementing a comprehensive curriculum driven by essential questions and understandings
- An increase in the use of standards set by students for their own work.

At this point, a few observations can be made about these benchmarks. First, the benchmarks are different for each design. Second, benchmarks serve to provide schools with a series of expectations for changes; these expectations did not exist in earlier phases. These benchmarks help explain the design to schools looking for some clarity as well as explain the process by which the school will change and the sequence of that process. Third, the benchmarks are largely process oriented and directed at the adult staff of the schools. They do not in general, though each team has some exceptions, indicate the level of student achievement or other student accomplishments that are expected and when they might be achieved. In this sense they are clearly implementation benchmarks and not achievement or outcome benchmarks.

While the development of the benchmarks is important, so too is the manner in which they are used. The variety among the teams can be consolidated into two approaches. AC and RW tend to use these benchmarks as the means by which the design team judges whether implementation has taken place. In other words, the benchmarks are for the team to use in assessing the school: Using these benchmarks, the team assesses implementation, provides feedback to the schools, and helps arrange further needed assistance.

In contrast, the other teams (ATLAS, CON, MRSH, NARE) provide the benchmarks to schools for the school's own self-assessment. (In fact, NARE had moved down this path prior to the other designs, in part because of its independent work with districts outside the NAS districts and in part because of its design philosophy of adopting best business practices.) In several cases the teams now provide guiding benchmarks that the schools further develop and adapt as their own. In this sense these teams use the benchmarks as part of a self-improvement process that the school enters into upon partnering with the team. ATLAS provides these across the pathway; that is, the pathway of schools must come together to assess the pathway's progress.

ELOB provides both types of benchmarks—design team implementation checks and ones the school can use.

CON alone uses these benchmarks to build the network of design-related schools. It established Critical Friends visits in the demonstration phase. During these visits teachers from other CON schools use benchmarks to judge the implementation effectiveness of a target school's design efforts. These visitors from other CON schools provide feedback and demand progress. ELOB is now following suit.

Measuring Progress on Student Outcomes

Assessment of implementation is needed to understand design team progress and effectiveness; measurement of changes in student outcomes is also necessary. Ideally, and certainly in the original proposals, each team thought to develop its own assessments keyed to design concepts or use some national-level authentic assessment regime to understand if performance had changed. As explained in Chapter Three, districts were not supportive of this approach. Each district had mandated testing regimes and was reluctant to put additional burdens on schools in terms of assessments. The districts told design teams that the district would hold the teams accountable for improvement on district-mandated tests. Furthermore, the cost of developing a design-specific assessment system put this out of reach of several teams.

Therefore, in all cases, evaluation of designs and much of the self-assessments of teams has been based on district test scores, not design-developed assessments. Several important exceptions exist. RW still uses its student-level assessments for student placement in curricular groups. NARE has a set of assessments it urges schools to use. CON and MRSH schools often use their assessments in modest forms. For understanding school-wide changes, however, most designs are forced to rely on district-mandated tests.

This reliance has a potentially undesirable result. As we saw in Chapter Three, some of these assessments might run counter to the principles of the designs. Thus, designs might use unaligned tests for their own self-assessments, which would make it difficult to do a reasonable self-assessment. Rather, the designs can only use these assessments to know if the design as implemented matches the content required of the district assessment. Just as problematic, some design teams did not adequately develop a capacity to track and understand the implications of these assessments.

Use of Assessment Tools by Teams as of 1998

True to its word, NAS has provided for an independent assessment of its efforts through the RAND evaluations. These evaluations were never intended and will not provide the detailed self-examination needed for teams to propel their efforts forward, nor are they intended to prove the effectiveness of each design on its own terms.

While teams developed some of the means for assessing implementation or for schools to assess their own implementation, it remains unclear how they have used this for self-improvement.

Most important, teams have been woefully lacking in the development of the means for their own self-assessment based on student outcomes. In a recent report by the American Institute for Research (1999), only one of the NAS teams was found to have developed strong or promising research evidence of an effect—ELOB. The Success for All reading component used by Roots and Wings was also found to have strong research and evidence of an effect. Until recently, however, Success for All was not considered a NAS design since it preexisted NAS. All others were found to be lacking this evidence. We note that many other comprehensive school designs also lack this evidence, especially those that are relatively new.

While newness provides a reason for not having developed this evidence, it cannot be seen any longer as an excuse. Without this type of assessment capability, teams will lack the information needed to improve as well as the information needed to convince schools of their effectiveness. Thus, while all teams recognize quality control as important, it is clear that development of this capability has not proceeded nearly far enough.

Two factors have limited its growth. Design teams are limited in the student outcome data they might collect to understand their progress, due to conflicting district policies. And design teams have been limited by their own lack of resources to develop more sophisticated assessments systems. Lacking both incentives from districts and funds from NAS, this data capability has not developed as originally foreseen.

Some progress might be forthcoming as teams now pay more attention to this issue. NAS is working jointly with teams to more systematically gather information about their performance and report it to the public.

IMPLICATIONS OF THE DEVELOPMENT OF IMPLEMENTATION STRATEGIES

In the early proposals and early work, the contribution of implementation support to the design concept was recognized but underdeveloped. Implementation assistance has grown considerably to include a rational selection process; specified committee structures, task forces, and learning groups within schools; formal assistance packages; and the beginnings of a quality control system. The manner of growth has been influenced tremendously by both the needs of teachers and the policy stances of districts.

Similar to other efforts, the NAS designs found that the introduction of the design into the school was crucial to eventual success. While it could be the case that some teachers could adopt practices and later come to believe in them, most teachers found the mandated approach of the districts to be off-putting and the selection process to be less than desirable. The teams have attempted to improve this process and the support materials to encourage informed choice on the part of teachers. However, district context and resources still heavily influence the process in each locale. Also, while some teams still require a high percentage of votes to proceed with implementation, they recognize that a small group of adamantly opposed teachers can derail the implementation effort in any school.

We draw from this the following implication: Strong positive support is not enough; the selection process must ensure the lack of a strong teacher-led backlash to design implementation.

All experiences of the design teams point to the need for a base of well-developed materials that explain the design and make clear the commitment teachers must make in implementation, but materials are not enough. Consistent with research on the importance of time for teachers (Purnell and Hill, 1992), teams must have schemes for schools to readily adopt to produce common time for teachers, time for curriculum development, time for significant and sustained staff development, and time for sharing at the school level to develop a community of practice. Time here means time during the regular school day for these interactions, but also refers to the need for sustaining these activities over long periods of time—several years.

District demands for immediate results, lack of resources dedicated to professional development, lack of incentives for teacher sharing, and policies that encourage the rapid turnover of teachers in schools undermined those efforts to provide time for reform. Just as importantly, so did the daily lives of teachers which, like others in the workforce, demand multiple roles and allow little time for working at innovation. Thus, even with the great deal of adaptation and growth on the parts of teams, the need for district-level support remains. The implication is that design assistance is not enough. District assistance is still needed and was missing in scale-up, despite NAS's efforts.

The teams have made strides in quality assurance through the significant development of benchmarks, which came about at least in part as an adaptation to the demands by districts and the clients. Districts have also limited the furtherance of this function because of their strong stance on mandated tests as the sole indicator of positive outcomes.

In sum, on the one hand we see that adaptation to client needs has been beneficial to the design concept by causing the growth of strong implementation strategies to support designs in schools. On the other hand, continued adaptation to conflicting district policies has increased the possibility of excessive local variation, especially when districts control the resources available to schools for buying implementation support or time resources in the schools. In addition, this adaptation has in some ways stunted the ability of designs to further develop due to the heavy reliance on district-mandated test data that might not align well with what designs are attempting to accomplish. Quality assurance within teams has not been at a fast enough pace to propel the designs further. The design teams are now addressing this issue, but a great deal of work remains.

A further implication, hinted at in our literature review, arises from this review of changes to implementation strategies. With this growth in assistance, it has become unclear whether the design is the intervention of interest, or whether it is the assistance, or whether it is both. NAS began with a working hypothesis that comprehensive designs would bring unity and cohesion to schools, and this would in turn improve student outcomes. Now teams have strong implementation strategies and provide schools with important generic assistance. At the same time, Chapter Three showed that many design elements have become less evident, with extreme local variation promoted and possible incoherence within the design. In short, there might be more assistance than design in the design-based assistance being received by schools.

Given these changes, it is now possible that any effects of the designs on student outcomes are due more to the implementation assistance than to the design, or lack of improvement might be due to the lack of design cohesion and not to poor assistance. We cannot provide evidence one way or the other, but we suggest that, given the evolution described, these are now reasonable hypotheses to be tested.

Chapter Five

CONCLUSIONS AND POLICY IMPLICATIONS

From the foregoing analysis, it is obvious that the portfolio of designs has changed, the designs themselves have changed, and strategies for implementation that were not in the original proposals have developed. These changes were driven by planned development of the teams; adaptations to teacher and student needs; adaptations to the policy environment; and learning from the teams. Teams did work to develop much stronger implementation strategies. Some of these adaptations and developments appear to have positively affected the concept of a design as both articulated and implemented, making the designs more adaptable to local circumstances, implementation more easily achieved, and the design elements more internally aligned with one another. Other changes raise questions concerning the ability to recognize a design-based school, given extensive local variation; the contribution of the design concept to internal program coherence at the school; and the ability of teams to further improve the designs. We summarize our findings first and then turn to implications.

NAS PORTFOLIO AND STRATEGY CHANGES

The design portfolio and strategy changes observed match the expectations set up in the literature review. Unforeseen funding concerns drove the reduction in number of design teams and designs. Two district-led teams suffered internal or local political situations that restricted their ability to develop strategies and practices central to their designs. Four teams, including the two led by districts, did not demonstrate to NAS's satisfaction an interest in or ability to scale up outside their local areas. NAS chose to eliminate from scale-up these four design teams and designs.

NAS then moved to establish the parameters of the scale-up phase, which included design teams working in ten jurisdictions that were chosen with NAS, based on the jurisdictions' presumed supportive environment. This approach indicated a growing understanding by NAS of the difficulties of school-level reform and how it had to be embedded in larger systemic reforms. But this approach also ensured that the success of the teams and their designs were dependent on the joint action of themselves, NAS, and the multiple players in the partner jurisdictions and raised the probability of strong effects from political factors, joint actions, and mutual adjustments.

CHANGES TO DESIGNS

While parts of the designs developed as planned, other parts changed in reaction to the above forces. Our analysis found that designs changed over this time period in several ways: planned development; response to the needs of students and teachers in the schools served; adaptation to conflicting policies, rules, and regulation; and complete reconceptualization of the design. We found the following:

All designs continued in their planned development. Schools and teams developed significant amounts of curriculum that could then be shared among new schools; improved the processes for the professional development of teachers; developed a process for cross-walking their standards to a district's standards; and developed diagnostic student assessments.

Interactions with students and teachers led to unplanned adaptations. The experiences of going to scale in large, poor, urban districts led to the adoption or development of basic literacy and numeracy programs and the development of processes to train teachers to develop rubrics for assessing student work against state or district standards. Lack of teacher time and capability led all teams to further develop their assistance packages and to develop curricular and other materials more suited to this group of teachers.

Interactions with existing policy environments resulted in further unplanned adaptations. Designs adapted significantly to the pressures posed by states, districts, schools, and unions to meet the existing regulatory, organizational, and cultural environment. The reality of working in the scale-up districts drove design teams to gradually lengthen implementation schedules, drop elements of design, or move from required activities to principles to be worked toward. The exception is the NARE design, which did not gradually adapt to district needs but held to its design, until it formally reconceptualized the entire design and dropped the old design.

Adaptation has led to extensive local variation among schools using the same design and potential incoherence in design-based schools. The accommodating stance taken by most designs in their newer versions of design documents allows significant variation in sites associated with a single team. When teams allow mandated standards, assessments, curriculum, and other professional development to substitute for their own, the coherence of the school's program is possibly lessened or remains as fragmented as before the use of the design. Allowing a large range of implementation of elements of designs instead of strong adherence to design principles also increases the probability that the schools will never attempt the full vision of the design and never achieve the student performance hoped for by the design teams.

DEVELOPMENT OF IMPLEMENTATION STRATEGIES

Over the last several years implementation assistance offered by design teams has grown considerably to include a selection process; specified committee structures, task forces, and learning groups within schools; formal assistance packages; and the beginnings of a quality control system. The manner of growth has been influenced tremendously by both the needs of teachers and the policy stances of districts.

NAS design teams found the introduction of the intervention into the school was crucial to the eventual success of the effort. The teams have attempted to improve this process and their support materials to encourage informed choice on the part of teachers. However, district context and resources still heavily influence the process in each locale, and the selection process must ensure not only strong teacher support but the lack of a small, but adamant backlash to the design.

The need for slack resources for reform was a major issue during the scale-up phase. Despite the growth in assistance and implementation strategies by the design teams, these assistance packages are limited by the slack resources available within the district for those undertaking reform. This lack of slack resources comes in many forms. Consistent with research (Purnell and Hill, 1992), teams must have readily adaptable schemes for schools to produce common time for teachers, time for curriculum development, time for significant and sustained staff development, and time for sharing at the school level to develop a community of practice. District demands for immediate results, lack of resources dedicated to professional development, lack of incentives for teacher sharing, and policies that encourage the rapid turnover of teachers in schools undermine these efforts to provide slack in the system for reform activities. The implication is that design assistance developed so far is not enough. District assistance in offering slack resources for innovation and improvement is needed and remains a hindrance to schools meeting the vision of the designs.

The teams have made strides in quality assurance through the significant development of benchmarks, which emerged at least in part as an adaptation to the demands by districts and the clients for accountability. However, districts have also inadvertently limited the furtherance of this function by insisting on one accountability measure—performance on mandated tests—which has influenced teams' development of assessment components. Teams have little incentive to develop unique tests or assessments geared to more complex performance expectations and little incentive to further advocate for curriculum and instruction that teaches more complex or interdisciplinary approaches than those measured by the mandated tests.

IMPLICATIONS

NAS began with a working hypothesis that comprehensive designs would bring unity and cohesion to schools, which would in turn improve student outcomes. Teams have developed stronger implementation strategies and provided schools with important generic assistance. They have further developed some design elements to meet the needs of students and teachers in the scale-up districts. At the same time, in order to ensure some level of acceptability, teams have attenuated certain design elements, promoted significant local adaptation, and possibly diluted the design coherence through acceptance of others' standards, assessments, and curriculum in design-based schools. Thus, it is now possible that any effects on student outcomes of the design-based assistance offered by a team are due more to the implementation assistance than to the actual implementation of a coherent design. Conversely, it is possible that lack of improvement in student performance observed in some "design-based schools" is due to the lack of design cohesion and not to poor assistance from teams. We cannot provide evidence one way or the other, but this review indicates that these are reasonable hypotheses to be considered.

We do not intend to draw some final judgment here but to warn of the possible danger that currently exists in too much adaptation or too much local variation and the implication for comprehensive school reform. There is a conflict at some point between creating break-the-mold schools based in design concepts and achieving high levels of implementation in large numbers of schools within and across many districts. This conflict develops especially when dealing with nonsupportive districts. Some of the evidence presented in this report points to the conclusion that the NAS district scale-up strategy led the designs toward that conflict. Should they continue scale-up and adaptation or should they move toward stricter definition and coherence? Or are there interventions that need to take place, especially at the district level, to avoid this possible dilution (Bodilly and Berends, 1999)?

We believe that the evidence points to the need for NAS and its teams to pay greater attention to and develop better understanding of important adaptation responses and their effect on:

- The meaning of school-based design and design coherence as a reform and its contribution to student performance. They must address what are the essential ingredients of the design concept.

- The nature of the design assistance package and implementation process and their contribution to student performance. They must address whether it is the process of implementation that is the contribution or the design or both.

- The necessary resources for reform implementation especially in terms of slack resources. They must address how these can be gained to enable the selection and implementation of coherent designs in schools.

- Government strategies to avoid dilution of essential design concepts and to promote effective assistance. They must address whether they should and how they could influence the policy process in positive ways to support their effort.

The federal government has already committed itself to the promotion and scale-up of comprehensive school reforms (and did so based on scant evidence of effectiveness (AIR, 1999)). The assumption behind this legislation is that school program coherence, based in explicit goals, standards, and accountability mechanisms, will lead to improved student performance. The CSRD in effect hypothesizes that one effective means for achieving the needed school coherence is the use of design-based assistance—that designs combined with external assistance will enable schools to significantly reduce fragmentation and increase effectiveness, thereby improving their students' performance. Behind this assumption is the assumption of some level of design coherence, high levels of implementation through external assistance, and application of slack resources including federal funds and strong district support.

RAND's work indicates several possible disconnects in the causative flow being hypothesized. First, in the development of NAS designs existing state standards, assessments, and accountability mechanisms often conflicted with principles of designs instead of providing important scaffolding for them. Design team adaptations to these state mandates sometimes resulted in less coherent designs and observed chaotic implementation. Second, in their development, design teams have faced weak district support and lack of slack resources for reform. Their adaptation has been to change designs to allow for different levels of implementation or combinations of different components of the designs to be determined at the local level. This approach can further dilute the coherence of the design both in principle and in actual implementation. In general then, attention has not been paid to the influence of states, districts, unions, and teachers in encouraging or discouraging the development of principles of design coherence during design development or during actual implementation. Neither has much attention been paid to the needs of different school populations and their impact on coherence (Bodilly and Berends, 1999).

We have seen that most NAS designs have changed significantly over time when faced with scale-up imperatives in NAS partner districts. We would expect that other designs going after CSRD funding will manifest phenomena similar to that of NAS designs. An ambitious drive for significant scale-up within a relatively short period of time will likely result in both planned development as well as concessions about design concepts unless district and other influences are channeled in positive directions. There is, however, no district, state, or federal strategy to affect this direction. In addition, it is likely that the newly developing design teams now coming into bloom will require significant influx of resources to develop implementation strategies, assistance packages, and supports. The federal policy provides somewhat for this.

As indicated by Mazmanian and Sabatier (1989), policy innovations do go through cycles of bloom, erosion and retrenchment, and then revitalization, depending on the attention being paid to them and competing priorities, etc. We might simply be documenting the first cycle of this type of phenomenon. However, if the next phase is to move from erosion to revitalization and growth, then policymakers must take certain steps. NAS by itself, a small business-oriented nonprofit, does not have the resources or influence to make all these changes come to pass.

If the federal government desires a test of the hypothesis inherent in the CSRD program outlined above, then the federal government, other governmental bodies, and others such as NAS should consider ways in which to protect designs from inappropriate dilution leading toward school program incoherence or determine how much coherence is effective. It should address the need for development of strong implementation strategies especially in the selection process. Remedies might include all of the following:

- Required three-year waivers from state and district standards, curriculum program mandates, and testing regimes for all schools gaining federal funds to enable them to implement a coherent design that can later be appropriately assessed against nondesign comparison schools and gradually adapted to the state regulatory environment.

- Federal support for the development and use of alternative assessment systems appropriate for judging design effectiveness aligned with their unique standards and curriculum.

- Consideration by districts of multiple assessment tools and outcomes for design-based schools and later for all schools if shown to be effective and efficient.

- Further federal or other support to design teams or third-party observers for documentation of design concepts, benchmarks for implementing the concepts, and evaluation of the implementation of the concepts.

- The development of more collaborative efforts at building district and state support for CSRD sites that ensures a supportive environment, especially one that promotes time for administrators and teachers to learn about the design, make an informed choice about which design to choose, and do the actual work of implementation.

- Recognition of the importance of changing structural problems in concert with adopting designs. Policy attention must be devoted to ending significant teacher turnover in low-performing schools through better pay, improved professional development, and true attempts at building a collegial community of learners.

American Institutes for Research, *An Educator's Guide to Schoolwide Reform*, Arlington, Va.: Educational Research Service, 1999.

Bardach, Eugene, *The Implementation Game*, Cambridge, Mass.: MIT Press, 1977.

Berends, Mark, *Assessing the Progress of New American Schools: A Status Report*, Santa Monica, Calif.: RAND, MR-1085-NAS, 1999.

Berends, Mark, Sheila Kirby, Scott Naftel, and Christopher McKelvey, *Implementation and Performance in New American Schools: Three Years After Scale-Up*, Santa Monica, Calif.: RAND, MD-1145-EDU, 2000.

Berman, Paul, and Milbrey McLaughlin, *Federal Programs Supporting Educational Change, Vol. IV: The Findings in Review*, Santa Monica, Calif.: RAND, R-1589/4-HEW, April 1975.

Bikson, Tora K., and J. D. Eveland, *Integrating New Tools into Information Work: Technology Transfer as a Framework for Understanding Success*, Santa Monica, Calif.: RAND, RP-106, 1992.

Bikson, Tora K., and J. D. Eveland, *Groupware Implementation: Reinvention in the Sociotechnical Frame*, Santa Monica, Calif.: RAND, RP-703, 1998.

Bikson, Tora K., Sally Ann Law, Martin Markovich, and Barbara T. Harder, *Facilitating the Implementation of Research Findings: A Summary Report*, Santa Monica, Calif.: RAND, RP-595, 1997.

Bodilly, Susan J., *Lessons from New American Schools' Scale-Up Phase: Prospects for Bringing Designs to Multiple Schools*, Santa Monica, Calif.: RAND, MR-942-NAS, 1998.

Bodilly, Susan J., and Mark Berends, "Necessary District Support for Comprehensive School Reform," *Hard Work for Good Schools, Facts Not Fads in Title I Reforms*, The Civil Rights Project, Cambridge, Mass.: Harvard University, 1999.

Bodilly, Susan J., S. W. Purnell, Kimberly Ramsey, and Sarah J. Keith, *Lessons from New American Schools Development Corporation's Demonstration Phase*, Santa Monica, Calif.: RAND, MR-729-NASDC, 1996.

Bodilly, Susan J., S. W. Purnell, Kimberly Ramsey, and Christina Smith, *Designing New American Schools: Baseline Observations on Nine Design Teams*, Santa Monica, Calif.: RAND, MR-598-NASDC, 1995.

Cuban, Larry, "Transforming the Frog into a Prince: Effective Schools Research, Policy, and Practice at the District Level," *Harvard Education Review*, Vol. 54, No. 2, May 1984.

Eveland, J. D., and Tora K. Bikson, *Work Group Structures and Computer Support: A Field Experiment*, Santa Monica, Calif.: RAND, N-2978-MF, 1989.

Fullan, Michael, *Change Forces the Sequel*, Philadelphia: Falmer Press, 1999.

Gandal, M., "Not All Standards Are Created Equal," *Educational Leadership*, Vol. 52, No. 6, 1995, pp. 11–21.

Gandal, M., *Making Standards Matter, 1996: An Annual Fifty State Report on Efforts to Raise Academic Standards*, Washington, D.C.: American Federation of Teachers, 1996.

Gitlin, Andrew, and Frank Margonis, "The Political Aspect of Reform: Teacher Resistance as Good Sense," *American Journal of Education*, No. 103, August 1995, pp. 377–405.

Glennan, Thomas K., Jr., *New American Schools After Six Years*, Santa Monica, Calif.: RAND, MR-945-NAS, 1998.

Goggin, Malcolm L., Ann Bowman, James Lester, and Laurence O'Toole, *Implementation Theory and Practice: Toward Third Generation*, New York: HarperCollins, 1990.

Huberman, Michael, and Mathew Miles, "Rethinking the Quest for School Improvement: Some Findings from the DESSI Study," *Teachers College Record*, Vol. 86, No. 1, Fall 1984.

Keltner, Brent, "Funding Comprehensive School Reform," Santa Monica, Calif.: RAND, IP-175, 1998.

Mazmanian, Daniel, and Paul Sabatier, *Implementation and Public Policy*, Lanham, Md.: University Press of America, 1989.

McDonnell, Lorraine, and Norton Grubb, *Education and Training for Work: The Policy Instruments and the Institutions*, Berkeley: National Center for Research on Vocational Education, University of California, R-4026-NCRVE/UCB, 1991.

McLaughlin, Milbrey, "Learning for Experience: Lessons from Policy Implementation," *Educational Evaluation and Policy Analysis*, Vol. 9, No. 22, Summer 1987, pp. 171–178.

McLaughlin, Milbrey, "The Rand Change Agent Study Revisited: Macro Perspectives and Micro Realities," *Education Researcher*, Vol. 19, No. 9, 1990, pp. 11–16.

Mickelson, Roslyn Arlin, and Angela L. Wadsworth, "NASDC's Odyssey in Dallas (NC): Women, Class, and School Reform," *Educational Policy*, Vol. 10, No. 3, September 1996, pp. 315–341.

Mirel, Jeffery, "School Reform Unplugged: The Bensenville New American School Project, 1991–1993," *American Educational Research Journal*, Vol. 31, No. 3, Fall 1994, pp. 481–518.

Mohrman, Susan, Edward Lawler, and Allan Mohrman, "Applying Employee Involvement in Schools," *Education Evaluation and Policy Analysis*, Vol. 14, No. 4, Winter 1992, pp. 347–360.

National Center for History in the Schools, *History Standards Project: National Standards for History*, 1996.

National Council of Teachers of Mathematics, *Curriculum and Evaluation: Standards for School Mathematics*, 1989.

National Science Teachers Association and the American Association for the Advancement of Science, *Benchmarks for Science Literacy; Project 2061*, New York: Oxford University Press, 1993.

New American Schools Development Corporation, *Designs for a New Generation of American Schools, Request for Proposals*, Arlington, Va., October 1991.

New American Schools Development Corporation, *Bringing Success to Scale: Sharing the Vision of New American Schools*, Arlington, Va., September 1995.

New Standards Project, *The New Standards Framework for Applied Learning—Discussion Draft*, Washington, D.C., 1994.

Pogrow, Stanley, "What Is an Exemplary Program, and Why Should Anyone Care? A Reaction to Slavin and Klein?" *Education Researcher*, October 1998, pp. 22–29.

Pogrow, Stanley, "The Unsubstantiated 'Success' of Success for All: Implications for Policy, Practice, and the Soul of Our Profession," *Phi Delta Kappan*, April 2000, pp. 596–600.

Pressman, Jeffrey, and Aaron Wildavsky, *Implementation*, Berkeley, Calif.: University of California Press, 1973.

Purnell, Susanna, and Paul Thomas Hill, "Time for Reform," Santa Monica, Calif.: RAND, R-4234-EMC, 1992.

Rosenberg, Jeffery, and Wade Horn, *How To Get Your Child Ready for School*, Indianapolis: Hudson Institute, 1994.

Rosenholtz, Susan, "Education Reform Strategies: Will They Increase Teacher Commitment?" *Schools as Collaborative Culture: Creating the Future Now*, New York: Falmer Press, 1990.

Schwarz, Paul, "Needed: School-Set Standards," *Education Week*, November 23, 1994, p. 44.

Slavin, R. E., "Design Competitions: A Proposal for a New Federal Role in Education Research and Development," *Education Researcher*, Vol. 26, No. 1, 1997a, pp. 22–28.

Slavin, R. E., Design Competitions and Expert Panels," *Education Researcher*, Vol. 26, No. 6, 1997b, pp. 21–22.

Slavin, R. E., "Rejoinder: Yes, Control Groups Are Essential in Program Evaluations: A Response to Pogrow," *Educational Researcher*, April 1999, pp. 36–38.

Slavin, R. E., "Research Overwhelmingly Supports Success for All," *Phi Delta Kappan*, Vol. 81, No. 9, May 2000, p. 720.

Slavin, Robert, Nancy Madden, Lawrence Dolan, and Barbara Wasik, *Every Child, Every School, Success for All*, Thousand Oaks, Calif.: Corwin Press, 1996.

Smrekar, Claire, "The Missing Link in School-Linked Services," *Educational Evaluations and Policy Analysis*, Vol. 16, No. 4, Winter 1994.

Spring, Joel, *The Sorting Machine: National Educational Policy Since 1945*, White Plains, N.Y.: Longman, 1988.

Stringfield, Samuel, and Amanda Datnow (eds.), *Education and Urban Society*, Vol. 30, No. 3, 1998.

University of Pittsburgh, Learning Research and Development Center, *New Standards Project, 1992–1995: A Proposal*, Pittsburgh, 1992.

Usdan, Michael, "Goals 2000: Opportunities and Caveats," *Education Week*, November 23, 1994, p. 44.

Warren Little, Judith, "Norms of Collegiality and Experimentation: Workplace Conditions of School Success," *American Educational Research Journal*, Vol. 19, No. 3, Fall 1982, pp. 325–340.

Warren Little, Judith, "Teachers as Colleagues," in *Schools As Collaborative Culture: Creating the Future Now*, New York: Falmer Press, 1990.

Weatherley, Richard, and Michael Lipsky, "Street-Level Bureaucrats and Institutional Innovation: Implementing Special Education Reforms," *Harvard Educational Review*, Vol. 47, No. 2, May 1977, pp. 171–197.

Wilson, James, *Bureaucracy: What Government Agencies Do and Why They Do It*, New York: Basic Books, 1989.

Wong, Kenneth, and Stephen Meyer, "Title I Schoolwide Programs: A Synthesis of Findings from Recent Evaluations," *Educational Evaluation and Policy Analysis*, Vol. 20, No. 2, 1998, pp. 115–136.

Yin, Robert, *Changing Bureaucracies*, Lexington, Mass.: Lexington Books, 1979.

Design Team Documents Cited

AC Proposal, *The College for Human Services Design Team Proposal to New American Schools Development Corporation*, February 14, 1992.

ATLAS Proposal, *ATLAS Communities, Authentic Teaching, Learning, and Assessment for All Students*, Theodore Sizer, James Comer, Howard Gardner, Janet Whitla, February 13, 1992.

ATLAS Communities, *Design Summary*, April 1, 1995.

CON Profile.

CON Proposal, *The Co-NECT School, a Design for a New Generation of American Schools*, Bolt Beranek and Newman, February 1992.

ELOB, "Fieldwork, an Expeditionary Learning Outward Bound Reader," Cambridge, Mass.: ELOB, Vol. 1, 1995.

ELOB: Grooms, Ain, *Annotated Bibliography of Learning Expedition*, Summer 1998.

ELOB Proposal, *Expeditionary Learning: A Design for New American Schools*, Outward Bound USA, February 14, 1992.

ELOB, *Guide for Planning a Learning Expedition, Expeditionary Learning Outward Bound*, Dubuque, Ia.: Kendall/Hunt Publishing Company, 1998.

MRSH, 1994.

MRSH, *Getting Your Child Ready for School*, Hudson Institute, 1995a.

MRSH, "Community Involvement Handbook," Nashville, Tenn., 1995b.

MRSH, "Essential Elements," Red folder.

MRSH Proposal, *The Modern Red Schoolhouse*, Hudson Institute, February 14, 1992.

NARE Proposal, *School—Systems—for the 21st Century*, National Center on Education and the Economy, February 1992.

RW Proposal, *Roots and Wings Universal Excellence in Elementary Education, A Collaborative Project, Center on Effective Schooling for Disadvantaged Students*, Johns Hopkins, Maryland State Department of Education, St. Mary's County Public Schools, February 15, 1992.